# HEALTH
# AND
# HAPPINESS

# HEALTH AND HAPPINESS

## Sri Swami Sivananda

**Published by**
THE DIVINE LIFE SOCIETY
P.O. SHIVANANDANAGAR—249 192
Distt. Tehri-Garhwal, Uttaranchal, Himalayas, India

Price ]  2006  [ Rs. 70/-

First Edition: 1950
Second Edition: 1965
Third Edition: 1984
Fourth Edition: 1996
Fifth Edition: 2001
Sixth Edition: 2006
[ 1,000 Copies ]

©The Divine Life Trust Society

ISBN 81-7052-034-7
ES 55

Published by Swami Vimalananda for
The Divine Life Society, Shivanandanagar, and
printed by him at the Yoga-Vedanta Forest Academy Press,
P.O. Shivanandanagar, Distt. Tehri-Garhwal, Uttaranchal,
Himalayas, India

*Dedicated to
Mother Prakriti, Nature,
Lord Dhanvantari,
The Asvini Kumaras,
And to every one, everywhere,
For Health, Longevity and
Happiness; Peace, Contentment
and Prosperity.*

SRI SWAMI SIVANANDA

# SRI SWAMI SIVANANDA

Born on the 8th September, 1887, in the illustrious family of Sage Appayya Dikshitar and several other renowned saints and savants, Sri Swami Sivananda had a natural flair for a life devoted to the study and practice of Vedanta. Added to this was an inborn eagerness to serve all and an innate feeling of unity with all mankind.

His passion for service drew him to the medical career; and soon he gravitated to where he thought that his service was most needed. Malaya claimed him. He had earlier been editing a health journal and wrote extensively on health problems. He discovered that people needed right knowledge most of all; dissemination of that knowledge he espoused as his own mission.

It was divine dispensation and the blessing of God upon mankind that the doctor of body and mind renounced his career and took to a life of renunciation to qualify for ministering to the soul of man. He settled down at Rishikesh in 1924, practised intense austerities and shone as a great Yogi, saint, sage and Jivanmukta.

In 1932 Swami Sivananda started the Sivanandashram. In 1936 was born The Divine Life Society. In 1948 the Yoga-Vedanta Forest Academy was organised. Dissemination of spiritual knowledge and training of people in Yoga and Vedanta were their aim and object. In 1950 Swamiji undertook a lightning tour of India and Ceylon. In 1953 Swamiji convened a 'World Parliament of Religions'. Swamiji is the author of over 300 volumes and has disciples all over the world, belonging to all nationalities, religions and creeds. To read Swamiji's works is to drink at the Fountain of Wisdom Supreme. On 14th July, 1963 Swamiji entered Mahasamadhi.

## MAHAMRITYUNJAYA MANTRA

ॐ त्र्यम्बकं यजामहे सुगन्धिं पुष्टिवर्धनम् ।
उर्वारुकमिव बन्धनान्मृत्योर्मुक्षीय माऽमृतात् ॥

Om Tryambakam Yajaamahe Sugandhim Pushtivardhanam,
Urvaarukamiva Bandhanaan-Mrityor-Muksheeya Maamritaat.

OM! I bow to that three-eyed Lord Siva who is full of sweet fragrance, who nourishes the human beings. May He free me from the bondage of Samsara and death, for the sake of Immortality, even as the cucumber is severed from its bondage (of the creeper).

**Note:** Repeat the above prayer at least 108 times daily. You will be protected from accidents and calamities. You will have a long life and a healthy body.

## CAUSES OF DISEASE

अत्यम्बुपानादतिसंगमाच्च दिवा च सुप्तेर्निशि जागरच्च ।
अत्याशनान्मूत्रपुरीषरोधात् षड्भिः किलैतैः प्रभवन्ति रोगाः ॥

Immoderate drinking of water, excessive venery, sleep by day, and wake by night, overloading the stomach, putting off answering nature's call,—these are the causes of illness.

Alcohol is a poison and proves highly deleterious to health by its injurious effect on the liver, nerves, blood-vessels and stomach. Excessive intake of water, too, is harmful.

Sexual excess shatters the nervous system altogether. The passions waste the nervous power.

Sleeping in the daytime is unnatural and it interferes with the sleep that naturally supervenes after day's hard labour.

Waking during the night is a strain on the nervous system.

Overloading the stomach upsets digestion and causes loss of tone.

Failure to answer the calls of nature in time poisons the system and exerts as bad an effect on the health of a man as an obstructed drain or a sewer and retention of solid refuse of a town have on the health of the community at large.

# HEALTH AND HAPPINESS

I am the God of Happiness,
    I simply make you smile:
I prove that life is worth living
    And that everything is worthwhile:
I force the failure to his feet
    And make the growler grin.
I am the God of Happiness:
    My name is Health and Happiness,
I am the God of luckiness;
    Observe my twinkling eye!
Success is sure to follow those
    Who keep me close by.
I make men strong and healthy—
    Who were quarrelsome and thin;
I am the God of luckiness:
    My name is Health and Happiness.

# PRAYER TO MOTHER NATURE

O Mother Nature! Salutations unto Thee!
Thou keepest the world show
Thou art all-merciful and kind
Thou art the Vitamins A, B, C, D, E,
Thou art the harmone
Thou art the body, mind and senses
Thou art the fruits, milk and nuts
Thou art energy, vigour and vitality
Thou art health, disease and Nature Cure
Thou art the Naturopath and Naturopathy
Thou art life, intelligence and consciousness
Thou art the bath and diet cure
Thou art the cell, gland and tissue
Thou art ultra-violet rays
Thou art the sun and the sun-cure
Thou art the curer and the patient
Thou art the herb and the juice
Thou art Power, motion and light
Thou art mineral and salt
O Mother Divine! Adoration unto Thee!
Reveal Thy true form unto me
Give me health and long life
Give me wisdom, light and power,
Let me behold Thee in all things
Let me remember Thee at all times
Let me see Thee in all forms
Let me feel Thy presence everywhere.
Shower Thy Grace on me
Help me to merge in Brahman—
Thy Consort, Lord and Partner
The Refuge, the Centre, the Goal of all.

# AN OPEN LETTER TO ALL

Immortal Self,
  Salutations and Adorations.

  You had enough of sense and sex-gratification in all your previous bodies of various animals. Animal life is meant for satisfaction of lower appetites of sex and tongue. But human life is meant for higher purpose. Why do you, O man, burn the sandalwood tree for purpose of charcoal? This human life is very precious, envied by even the gods. One life lost means one golden opportunity to become GOD is lost.

  Fight bravely in this battle of life. Arm yourself with the shield of discrimination and sword of dispassion. March forward courageously. Yield not to temptations. Meditate on the Inner self regularly. You will enter the illimitable domain of eternal bliss and everlasting peace. You will build up the life of calm, strength, repose and peace.

  *Therefore, be earnest, be sincere, be eager to have Satsanga with Mahatmas and do Nama Sankirtan for attaining God-consciousness.*

May the Lord bless you,

*Sivananda*

# CONTENTS

Sri Swami Sivananda . . . . . . . . . . . . . . . . . . . vii
Mahamrityunjaya Mantra . . . . . . . . . . . . . . . viii
Causes of Disease . . . . . . . . . . . . . . . . . . . . . ix
Health and Happiness . . . . . . . . . . . . . . . . . . x
Prayer to Mother Nature . . . . . . . . . . . . . . . . xi
An Open Letter to All . . . . . . . . . . . . . . . . . xii

## Chapter I

What Is Health? . . . . . . . . . . . . . . . . . . . . . . 3
Health Is a Great Treasure . . . . . . . . . . . . . . 3
Necessity for Good Health . . . . . . . . . . . . . . 6
Means for Good Health . . . . . . . . . . . . . . . . 7
Health and Longevity . . . . . . . . . . . . . . . . . . 8
Health and Long Life . . . . . . . . . . . . . . . . . 9
Chief Causes that Impair Good Health . . . . 10
Vital Facts about Health . . . . . . . . . . . . . . . 12
Health and Happiness . . . . . . . . . . . . . . . . . 13
Health and Hygiene . . . . . . . . . . . . . . . . . . . 15

## Chapter II

Nature Cure and Health . . . . . . . . . . . . . . . 17
Fasting in Nature Cure . . . . . . . . . . . . . . . . 18
Fasts and Their Importance . . . . . . . . . . . . 18
Antidotes for Indigestion . . . . . . . . . . . . . . 20
Health and the Elements . . . . . . . . . . . . . . 21
Sunlight and Health . . . . . . . . . . . . . . . . . . 23

| | |
|---|---|
| Bath | 27 |
| Sleep | 27 |
| Practical Aids to Sound Sleep | 28 |

### Chapter III

| | |
|---|---|
| Diet and Health | 31 |
| Fruits and Health | 35 |
| Milk and Health | 37 |
| Between Meat and Milk (A Dialogue) | 38 |
| Health, Hygiene and Diet | 40 |
| Health Menu | 41 |
| Shun Onion Pakkoda | 41 |

### Chapter IV

| | |
|---|---|
| Discovery of Vitamins | 44 |
| Classification of Vitamins | 46 |
| Dietetic Instructions | 47 |
| Mysterious Vitamins in Food | 48 |
| Dietetic Value of Vitamins | 49 |
| Vitamins and Health | 52 |
| Story of Vitamin A | 59 |
| Tale of Vitamin B | 64 |
| Vitamin B-2 or G | 69 |
| Vitamin C (Analysed) | 72 |
| Vitamin D (Analysed) | 76 |
| Vitamin E (Analysed) | 82 |
| The Story of Vitamins | 82 |

### Chapter V

| | |
|---|---|
| Dietetic Principles | 86 |
| Articles of Food | 88 |

## Chapter VI
Care of the Eyes ................ 91
Blindness and Its Causes ........... 91
Anatomy of the Eye .............. 92
Care of the Eyes ................ 93
Conjunctivitis ................... 104
Cataract ....................... 105
Glaucoma ...................... 105
Errors of Refraction .............. 106
Eyesight of Indians ............... 107

## Chapter VII
Physical Culture .................. 109
Physical Culture in Bed ........... 111
Suryanamaskara Technique .......... 114
Physical Culture for Babies ......... 116
Massage and Health .............. 117
Daily Electric Massage ............ 118

## Chapter VIII
Home Treatment of Diseases ........ 120

## Chapter IX
Ten Commandments .............. 128
Twenty-six Precepts ............... 128
Healing the Sick ................. 130
Yoga for Health ................. 131
Vedanta for Health ............... 133
Health and Astrology ............. 138
Vedantic Compressed Tablet ........ 138
Vedantic Vitamin ................ 139

Vedantic Beverage ................ 140
Vedantic Tonic ................. 140
Fattening and Thinning of 3 Bodies ..... 141
Havan for Curing Tuberculosis ........ 141
Divine Namapathy ............... 144
Moksha Rasayana ................ 145
An Adhyatmic Prescription .......... 146

## Chapter X
See Good in Everything ............ 148
Rules for Preservation of Health ....... 151
How to Keep Healthy ............. 153
The Cause of Ailments and the Cure .... 154
Use Your Commonsense ............ 155
Back to Nature ................. 156
Simple Nature Cure .............. 157
Influence of Thoughts on Health ...... 159
Soil and Its Influence on Health ....... 160
Influence of Colour on Health ........ 162
How to Become a Centenarian? ....... 164
The Best .................... 164
Song of Vibhuti Yoga ............. 165
Tact at the Chemist's ............. 165
Domestic Medicine Chest .......... 167

*Health and Happiness*

# Chapter I

## WHAT IS HEALTH?

What is health? It is that state of equilibrium of the three humours of the body, viz., *Vata, Pitta* and *Kapha* (wind, bile and phlegm), wherein the mind and all the organs of the body work in harmony and concord and man enjoys peace and happiness and performs his duties of life with comfort and ease.

Health is that condition in which man has good digestion, good appetite, a normal breathing and normal pulse, good quantity and quality of blood, strong nerves and a calm mind, a sound mind in a sound body, a free movement of the bowels, normal state of urine, rosy cheeks, shining face and sparkling eyes.

Health is that state in which a man jumps, sings, smiles, laughs, whistles and moves about hither and thither with joy and ecstasy. It is that condition in which he can think properly, speak properly and act with alacrity, nimbleness and vigilance.

Health is that state in which a man sleeps well, digests his food well, is quite at ease, is free from any kind of disease or uneasiness. When you are in a state of perfect health, all the organs, viz., heart, lungs, brain, kidneys, liver, intestines, work in perfect harmony and concord and discharge their functions satisfactorily. The pulse-rate and the rate of respiration are in perfect order. The bodily temperature is normal. This state is coveted by all. A life with good health is a great blessing indeed.

## HEALTH IS A GREAT TREASURE

Good health is a valuable asset to man. It is a great treasure. It bestows happiness and prosperity. Health is essential to happiness. Health is not merely absence of disease. It includes the full development of physical, mental and spiritual powers of a man. Health is a condition of physical and mental well-being: a normal state of body and mind in which all parts and organs perform their functions regularly, easily and satisfactorily and are free from disease, pain and weakness. A person who is endowed with good health, digests his food well, sleeps soundly and does his daily work satisfactorily. He is ever joyful and energetic. You should have a clear idea of what disease is and how it is caused. Only then will you be able to prevent a disease. Diseases can be averted if you understand the biological laws which govern life, the rules of health and hygiene and the importance of cleanliness. A general knowledge of the laws of health would help considerably in preventing sickness and death and improving the health of the people.

Of every hundred deaths occurring in India, Europe and other countries, sixty are said to be due to disease, which can be, to a very large extent, if not altogether, prevented, if the people are only wise and will take to those measures advocated by sanitary science.

Some persons are born with sound, healthy bodies: unfortunately others are not. How do you account for this? The doctrine of Karma will give you the best answer. Those who did good actions in their previous births get sound, healthy and strong bodies: those who did wicked actions obtain unhealthy weak bodies.

Many people make themselves ill by eating too much and by not eating the right thing at the right time. What are the ordinary things around you which help to keep you in good health? They are the Sun, fresh air and pure water. Sunlight helps growth and gives vigour. Breathe pure air, bask in the Sun, eat good nutritious wholesome food, drink pure water and observe cleanliness; you will possess a high standard of health, vim, vigour and vitality.

Life here is a continuous battle. It is a never-ending adventure. There are dragons to be destroyed. You will have to wage war with the enemies of health, viz., impure water, bad ventilation, overwork, unwholesome food, disease-germs, domestic pests such as flies, mosquitos, the rats and the fleas. You are surrounded on all sides by invisible foes—pathogens, microbes and bacteria. You should certainly learn all that you can about your enemies, their ways, habits and strength. In some cases you will have to attack them directly. In some other cases you must starve them out. You must adopt the most up-to-date weapons which modern sanitary science and preventive medicines have given you. You must tap your resources in every possible way.

Public health is not a matter that solely concerns Sanitaria, Municipalities or Health Departments. Every citizen, every individual, is directly and intimately concerned in the preservation of the health and welfare, not only of himself but, of the community as a whole.

Most of the diseases which are preventable are produced by some specific germs which are carried by air or water or food or clothing or other insects. A study of the life-history of these disease-causing germs and of the methods to exterminate them will be extremely helpful for the health and welfare of the community. Impure air, impure water, infected food, uncleanliness of houses and their surroundings, improper or bad disposal of excretion, play a vital part in the dissemination of disease.

Every individual must be educated in the science of hygiene and sanitation, so that he may be able to appreciate the value of sanitation, not only for his own health but also for that of the community at large.

The child must be protected before birth by antenatal precautions. The health and well-being of the child is the primary foundation of its education. Pregnant and nursing mothers must also be well protected. Maternity and child welfare centres must be established in each *taluk* and district. People must be protected from diseases like smallpox, plague, cholera, typhoid, etc., by taking recourse to artificial immunity through injection of vaccines.

May you all possess good health and vitality by observing the rules of health and hygiene and by the study of the science of sanitation and preventive medicine!

## NECESSITY FOR GOOD HEALTH

What is the earthly use of wealth and possessions, if a man cannot eat well on account of diseases of the stomach, if he cannot walk on account of rheumatism or paralysis, if he cannot see the beautiful scenery of nature on account of cataract or defective vision, if he cannot copulate on account of impotency? One great thinker says, "Give me health and a day, and I will make the pomp of emperors ridiculous." Life without good health is a miserable condition, even if one is the lord of the whole earth.

We should have good health to achieve the four kinds of Purushartha, viz., Dharma, Artha, Kama and Moksha (righteousness, wealth, desire and liberation). Without good health, you can hardly expect success in any walk of life. Even for spiritual pursuits good health is a prerequisite. Without good health you cannot penetrate into the hidden depths of the vast ocean of life within and attain the final beatitude of life. Without good health you cannot wage war against the turbulent senses and the boisterous mind.

Good health is your greatest asset. Without good health you cannot achieve anything. Without good health you cannot do any public service. Without good health you cannot pray and meditate. Without good health you cannot do Asanas and Pranayamas. This is the reason why scriptures declare that this body is a boat to cross this ocean of Samsara with, an instrument for doing virtuous deeds and attaining Moksha. That is the reason why in Charaka Samhita you will find: *"Arogyam Moolam Uttamam*—Health is the best thing in this world."

What is that precious thing that make life worth living? It is health. Will you sing today the song of *"Sariram Adyam Khalu Dharmasadhanam*—Body is indeed the foremost essential thing for the attainment of the goal of human existence (in other words, it is verily the first important means in the accomplishment of the object of human life)." Charaka Maharshi says in his Samhita, *"Dharmarthakamamokshanam arogyam moolamuttamam, Rogastasyaapahartarah sreyaso jivitaya cha*—Health is the best cause of virtue, wealth, enjoyment and emancipation, and is the blessedness of life. Diseases are the destroyers of health."

## MEANS FOR GOOD HEALTH

Good physical health can be achieved and maintained by observing rigidly the laws of Health and the Rules of Hygiene, by taking wholesome, light, substantial, easily digestible, nutritious, bland food or Sattvic diet, by inhaling pure air, by regular physical exercise, by daily cold bath, by observing moderation in eating, drinking, etc. Good mental health can be attained and maintained by Japa, meditation, Brahmacharya, practice of Yama, Niyama and right conduct, right thinking, right feeling, right speaking and right action, Atma Vichara, change of thought, relaxation of mind by letting the mind dwell on pleasant thoughts, mental recreation and the practice of cheerfulness.

The whole universe, from the mighty Sun to the tiniest atom, is controlled by law. There is perfect order everywhere. The Sun performs its duties quite regularly. It rises at the proper time and sets at the proper time. The stars and planets revolve in an orderly manner. They are governed by laws. There are laws in the mental plane. There are laws of physics, of astronomy, of mathematics. There are laws of hygiene and health which govern our own being. In the vast universe, man alone is the breaker of laws and the violator of rules. He is the single example of lawlessness and discord. He wilfully disregards the laws of health, leads a life of dissipation and then wonders why he suffers from diseases and disharmony! He deliberately ignores the rules of hygiene and right living and then weeps when he is ailing from an incurable malady.

How wonderful is this magical machine—the human body, the moving temple of God or the chariot for the soul! Mother Prakriti has exhibited her marvellous skill and maximum dexterity in constructing this marvellous machine. If you seriously ponder for a while over the structure and working of this wonderful machine that is our body, you will be struck with awe and wonder.

Everyone of you should possess some elementary knowledge of diseases and their treatment with common medicines and their uses, of physiology which treats of the functions of the different organs of the body, of anatomy which deals with the structure of the human frame, of first aid to the injured. If you are endowed with this knowledge, you can help yourself as well as the suffering humanity at large to some extent. This knowledge will help you in emergencies, before you are able to get hold of a doctor. Have a knowledge of the important points for preserving health, for giving first-aid to the injured, for treating cases of poisoning.

Study of anatomy and physiology, hygiene and the science of dietetics, which will help you to keep the body in a healthy and strong condition so that all its machinery may work harmoniously, must be your first study. You have ignored the laws of health and the rules of hygiene. Hence you have a poor health, poor physique and a dilapidated frame.

Regular practice of Yogic exercises or Yoga Asanas even for fifteen minutes a day will keep you quite fit and soon make you hale and hearty. You will have abundant energy, muscular strength and nerve-power, a charming personality and will live long.

## HEALTH AND LONGEVITY

He who drinks and has no thirst,
Or eats and has no hunger,
He who does not take any exercise,
Suffers illness and dies young.

He who wastes much the vital fluid,
He who uses tobacco,
He who takes heavy dinners,
Suffers illness and dies young.

He who drinks butter-milk,
He who eats tomatoes and lemons,
He who walks three miles daily,
Is healthy and attains longevity.

He who is moderate in everything,
He who basks in the Sun,

He who takes cold bath,
Is healthy and attains longevity.

He who is ever busy,
He who talks a little,
He who drinks water in the early morning,
Is healthy and attains long life.

He who takes spinach or Palak,
He who gets up when he is still hungry,
He who observes silence during eating,
Is healthy and attains long life.

He who fasts and meditates,
He who eats to live,
He who takes to Nature-cure,
Is healthy and attains immortality.

## HEALTH AND LONG LIFE

Observe the laws of health,
Attend to the rules of hygiene,
Prevention is better than cure,
Nip the malady in its bud.

Masticate the food thoroughly,
Have a balanced diet,
Take moderate food,
Avoid late supper at night.

Bask in the Sun for a while,
Run in the open air,
Have a long walk,
Do Danda and Kasrat.

Avoid liquor and intoxicants,
Have simple living and high thinking,
Take cold bath in the morning,
Lead a life of continence.

Diseases are the destroyers of health,
Health is the means for attaining the goal,
Keep the body healthy and strong,
Qualify yourself as your own doctor.

*Sariramadyam Khalu Dharmasadhanam,*
Have a knowledge of the diseases and symptoms,
And ward off the troubles and diseases,
Lead a life of ease and happiness,
Nurse the sick for getting Chitta-Suddhi,
And attain Eternal Bliss and Immortality.

Fast once in a month,
Give up salt on Sundays,
Keep the bowels open,
Get help from nature.

Go to bed early,
Rise up early,
Pray fervently,
Meditate regularly.

## CHIEF CAUSES THAT IMPAIR GOOD HEALTH

The main causes that impair good health are as follows:

(1) Pessimistic thoughts, (2) Fear of disease, (3) Lack of proper food, (4) Overwork, (5) Working late at night and (6) Various kinds of anxieties and worries.

***Pessimistic Thoughts:*** It is useless to harbour pessimistic thoughts, because the Almighty Lord has endowed man with the faculty of reasoning and the power of rising superior to all undesirable elements and tiding over uncongenial circumstances. Pessimistic thoughts not only make a man miserable and helpless, but have also a very adverse effect upon his mind and body and thus impair his health. He should always read inspiring things that cheer him up and pour life into his being, and also follow the footsteps of those who have triumphed over all trying circumstances. He should study the teachings of Sri Sankara, Dattatreya and Vasishtha.

***Fear of Diseases:*** God is always good and kind to one and all. What He does, He does always for good. A man learns more by experience than by mere precepts, and hence God sends difficulties to give lessons to mankind. The duty of man is, therefore, to face the difficulties boldly and perform his duties rightly. We are liable to suffering much from diseases if we

## CHIEF CAUSES THAT IMPAIR GOOD HEALTH

entertain fear of them. If we are bold enough, diseases can do us no harm.

***Lack of proper kind of food:*** Proper kind of food is a hard problem for the poor and the middle class men. The only way is to find out a solution to get the utmost benefit through the food which is available within their scanty means. For this purpose one should read literature on economic and nutritious food and arrange one's diet accordingly. There are good books on this subject in the vernacular languages; so, one need not go in for costly English books on the subject.

***Overwork:*** One should observe regularity in all one's duties and work which one has to perform. Wasting time for many days and working hard for a few days to make up puts a strain on the functions of the body; and heartache, dizziness and constipation are the result. One should always manage to take a little rest for a few minutes in the intervals of his various kinds of work and business. Working late hours at night can be avoided if a man manages to work till 10-11 p.m. and again after 3 a.m. in the morning hours. This method of work is far better and healthier than working till 1 or 2 a.m. in the night.

***Worries and Anxieties:*** They are very troublesome, and it is a Herculean task to overcome them. A man should try to meet them boldly and confidently, as it is within his power to do so. The best way to tide over them is to have full faith in God and His goodness. One should read the lives of saints and Bhaktas. They tell us that God sends these difficulties to test us and to purify our Karmas or actions in the previous life. All Scriptures show that even those whom God Almighty loved most were not free from cares and anxieties.

The difficulties and anxieties arising from poverty, lack of food, clothing and shelter, were shared by many a devotee of God. Even Hanuman, who was most beloved of Rama, had to face many difficulties even in doing Sri Rama's work, i.e., search for Sita. There is no other royal road to tide over them than to rely upon God and bear the natural consequences, keeping in mind that only Truth succeeds in the end. A person who is really devoted to the Lord never fears any difficulty. He finds God's Grace even in calamities which he has to suffer.

## VITAL FACTS ABOUT HEALTH

Though we boast ourselves to be civilised men, yet when the question of food comes, we make many imperceptible blunders.

The English system of taking food and breakfasts often and often is not compatible with the tropical climate of our country.

By taking cooked and concentrated foods with spices and condiments, we fill our belly with denatured food, and hence this degeneration in the physique of the youths of the 20th century.

We cannot change our age-long habits all of a sudden, and so we must have some compromise.

We should take some sort of exercise such as a morning walk or some abdominal gymnastics or Surya-Namaskaras or Asanas, at least two of them, i.e., Paschimottanasana and Sarvangasana.

We should take a morning bath either in hot or cold water.

We should have no breakfast—only a cup of milk or the juice of a lemon, an orange, tomato, in a cup of hot or cold water, after bath. Instead of milk, buttermilk will do. If nothing is available, a cup of hot or cold water will suffice.

We should not discard our usual meal in the morning, but should avoid fried and spiced food and sweets as far as practicable.

In the afternoon, instead of tea or coffee, we can take one or two fruits of a cheap quality available in the season.

Our evening meal should consist mainly of fruits and vegetables and milk or buttermilk.

The evening meal should be finished before 7 or 8 p.m.

We should go to bed between 10 and 11 p.m.

Fruits and vegetables which are Sun-cooked are the elixir of life and are nature's remedies. Animals living on Sun-cooked food have more strength and seldom fall sick!

Once a week we should have two meals of fruits, milk and vegetables only.

We should not entertain pessimistic thoughts. God is always good. The apparent difficulties which we have to face in life are for our progress, and we must pray to God for means and measures to overcome them. Before going to bed, we must bring the image of our favourite deity before our mind's eye and pray to God fervently to give us health, wealth and power to fight the battle of life successfully.

Occasional fasts are as essential as occasional feasts, to correct our errors against natural life, which are often inevitable. An occasional use of enema or castor oil, or any vegetable laxative, is necessary to clean our bowels, when we feel constipated.

Lastly, when we begin to take our usual meals of cereals, we should observe the following rules, as far as practicable.

Starches, fats, green vegetables, sugars can be taken together, as they require either an alkaline or natural medium for their digestion.

Proteins, fats, green vegetables and acid fruits may be taken together.

But starches and proteins, starches and acid fruits should not be eaten together.

It is a golden rule to take fruits in the morning and a silver rule to take them in the afternoon. Fruits may be taken alone. Only a little lemon juice may be added to give relish to our food. Buttermilk can be taken after meals or an hour or two after meals.

All these rules are for persons whose digestion is not good, and the number of such persons is legion. Only a very few persons of robust health can digest any kind of food and can overcome any irregularity in food by their strenuous work.

## HEALTH AND HAPPINESS

1. Health is certainly more valuable than money, because it is by health that money is procured. Health is wealth.

2. Without health there is no true beauty. You may have good features and complexion, but you cannot be called beautiful without radiant health.

3. Regularity in the hours of rising and retiring, moderation in all things, simple and nutritious diet, temperance, regular exercise, etc., go a long way to the attainment of health and longevity.

4. Sattvic food (good, wholesome food) rich in vitamins or a well-balanced diet, systematic practice of Asanas and Pranayama, right and simple living and right thinking, are the important requisites for the preservation of health and the attainment of a high standard of vigour and vitality.

5. Proper elimination is as important as a correct diet. Even when the right food is eaten, good health will not be enjoyed unless waste matter is properly removed from the system. You must have a good motion daily in the early morning. Drink sufficient quantity of water and flush the kidneys. You will enjoy good health.

6. Control your temper and tongue. You will have good health and long life.

7. You can have a healthy and beautiful body if you are regular in your habits and take a proper diet, sufficient exercise, etc.

8. For good health, an adult should take 6 glasses (or 1 lb. measure) of water daily in addition to water taken in the form of food. This is sufficient to flush the body and to meet all internal needs.

9. He who has health has strength, cheerfulness, vim, vigour and vitality. He who has hope, vigour and cheerfulness has everything.

10. Do not overload the stomach. The secret of being always healthy and happy is to be a little hungry all the time.

11. Health is the harmony of the whole man, of body, mind and spirit.

12. If the mothers are happy, the homes are happy; if the homes are happy, the villages are happy; if the villages are happy, the nation is happy. That is the fullest joy of independence.

13. Cheerfulness is the best mental and physical tonic. If you

are cheerful, the cells, tissues and nerves are also cheerful and healthy. Cheerfulness expands the heart and the brain, and fills the system with harmony and peace. Therefore be cheerful and joyful.

14. Cheerfulness and contentment are greater beautifiers and are more famous preservers of good looks than expensive cosmetics.

15. Laughter may justifiably be said to be a panacea for all the ills to which human flesh is heir.

16. Cheerfulness is the best tonic. It bestows good physical and mental health. Therefore be always cheerful.

## HEALTH AND HYGIENE

1. Your lack of health today is due to your ignorance and violation of the laws of health and hygiene during the past years.

2. You suffer in health and sleep because you get up from your bed many hours after the rising of the Sun and live in artificial light after the Sun has set.

3. You do not observe any regularity in your times for eating and sleeping and therefore tax your nerves and digestive apparatus unnecessarily.

4. The laws for the preservation of health should receive your foremost and first consideration. The laws of health are the laws of nature. These cannot be violated with impunity.

5. The well-being of a people depends more on perfect nutrition and efficient sanitation than on anything else.

6. The mouth is the gateway to the body and, in a very great measure, the largest entrance for the dreaded diseases, infections and maladies to get into our bodies.

7. Take simple food. Be moderate in eating. Take enough exercise. Be systematic in all things. If you feel uneasy and unwell, fast till you are well again. Take a little lemon juice in water.

8. Microbes or germs multiply very quickly. Under favourable conditions, a single germ that causes cholera or typhoid fever can give rise to a million germs in a few hours.

9. A drop of blood is the most wonderful thing in the world. Look at it through the microscope. It will reveal to you most astounding things. You will behold white cells, red cells, etc.

10. One-third of the heart lies on the right side and two-thirds on the left.

11. Cleanliness is next to Godliness. The clothing worn next to the skin should be changed and washed daily. This is very important from the hygienic viewpoint.

12. Faulty elimination is most common due to constipation or inactivity of the bowels. This is an exceedingly common condition today, on account of faulty habits of eating and living. Inactivity of the liver and the kidneys is often associated with this complaint.

13. He who observes the rules of health and hygiene, who is moderate in eating, drinking and other things, who is regular in his prayer, Japa, meditation, etc., who is free from jealousy, pride and hatred, who observes Brahmacharya is free from diseases. He is healthy and attains longevity.

## Chapter II

## NATURE CURE AND HEALTH

1. Do not run to the doctor every time you feel an ache or pain. Endeavour to qualify yourself as your own doctor, learn something about Nature's remedies. Nature's remedies will save you many a doctor's bill.

2. Every system has its own drawbacks or defects. But Naturopathy stands unrivalled, because Mother Nature acts as a kind and able physician here. No foreign matter is introduced into the system. Nature's agencies are utilised. Naturopathy is the divine system of treatment.

3. If a bye-law can be passed forbidding any talk about diseases for a week, the general health of the people will surely improve.

4. Fasting confers good health and longevity. It gives rest to all internal organs. It is the law of safety and of cure. Observe a complete fast on Ekadasi. Do not take even a drop of water.

5. Fasting is the supreme medicine. It cures many diseases. Therefore fast on Ekadasi at least.

6. Fasting has in numberless cases restored health when everything else has failed.

7. Break the fast taking fruit juice. Squeeze the juice of 2 or 3 oranges. If these are not available, you can take carrot juice.

8. Always be cheerful. Cultivate divine virtues. Take delight in selfless service. Sleep well. Take good rest. Take exercise in the open air. Sleep and live in well-ventilated rooms. Take cold bath in the early morning. Avoid late hours at night in going to sleep and in taking food. You need not go to any doctor, dentist, or X-ray specialist. You will enjoy beautiful health, poise, peace and happiness.

9. Live with nature. Use herbs and greens. Avail yourself of

the healing agencies of nature in the Sun, air, water, earth, fasting, herbs, etc.

## FASTING IN NATURE CURE

### I. General:

Fast is a curative measure of great importance. Short fasts upto 3 days can be taken without the help of any expert. For minor ailments, fasting for a day or two will do. Fasts for longer periods may be necessary to cure diseases of long-standing nature. During this naturopathic treatment, enema should be used daily to keep the bowels clean.

### II. Details on fasting—(Guidance):

Fast for a day, taking only the juice of a lemon, orange or mosambi, in a glass of water, three or four times a day.

For the next two days, take three meals of available fruits (except banana). Drink water mixed with juice of a lemon or orange.

For the next four days, along with the above fruits take a cup or two of milk (at each meal).

Thus the general treatment for some chronic ailment will be:

|     | Fast    | Fruit diet | Milk & Fruits | Total   |
| --- | ------- | ---------- | ------------- | ------- |
| (A) | 1 day   | 2 days     | 3 days        | 1 week  |
| (B) | 2 days  | 4 days     | 6 days        | 2 weeks |
| (C) | 3 days  | 6 days     | 12 days       | 3 weeks |

and so on.

After the above, the patient should have his usual meal in the day and take only fruits and milk at night as long as he can.

### III. External Treatment:

Cold-pack may be applied for pain in any part of the body; if the pain is unbearable, hot-water pack may be used.

## FASTS AND THEIR IMPORTANCE

Man's foremost duty is to do Sadhana for the realisation of God. For Sadhana a sound body and a sound mind are most essential. Fasts help a great deal in keeping the body in the best state of health. With all the best possible precautions, it is very

## FASTS AND THEIR IMPORTANCE

difficult to avoid committing mistakes in regard to the food that we take. A man with a great self-control may be moderate in food; but there are various other causes which he cannot avoid and thus his health gets impaired.

If there is the least symptom of disease in the body, it is a signal to fast for a day or two. Animals which depend only upon nature fast naturally if there is any disease, and cure themselves by natural means, e.g., Sunlight and fresh air, fasts and rest.

Cold, headache, slight feverishness, a little cough, loaded colon, are some of the signs of diseases, which, if neglected in the beginning, may take a serious form. To avert this impending danger, our Sastras have enjoined fasts on Ekadasi, Pradosha, Sivaratri, Poornima, Amavasya, on particular days in the week for the propitiation of particular deities. One should observe fast on any one of these days. But, as few persons are now in the habit of keeping the Indian Almanac, they may observe fasts on any weekday as it suits their work and convenience.

In the present circumstances, it is very, very difficult to fast without taking anything except water, without some practice. So, we must follow the golden mean of taking the juice of two or three fruits mixed with a considerable quantity of water. No solid food or fleshy fruits should be taken on that day. This kind of fast is good for preservation of health.

Really fast is a fast-curing agent for many of the ailments. It gives some rest to the stomach, and eliminates toxins from the body. It cleanses the body and thus makes it more energetic. It can cure many diseases. Much care is required in observing long fasts. They should be observed under the guidance of an expert; otherwise, if there is any mistake in their observance, there is every possibility of more harm than good being done to the system. Two or three days' fasts can be observed without the guidance of an expert; but the daily use of enema during the fasts, and for a day or two afterwards, is necessary.

*Short Fast Regime:* First day—Juice of an orange or Mosambi or lemon, mixed with a glass of water, 2 or 3 times. Second day—the same procedure may be followed, 3 or 4 times. Third day—You may take the juice as stated above, plus a cup of milk in the noon and at bedtime. Fourth day—You may take rice and milk for morning meals, and fleshy fruits for your evening meals, and also a cup of milk at bedtime. Fifth day—You may take your usual meal of Rotti, Dal and vegetables.

In this age, when there is a great lack of self-control, a weekly fast on any day, living on fruit juice, is much better and convenient; and this should be necessarily observed. Even this will be found difficult for many persons; so a half-day fast should invariably be observed by all persons. They should take fruit-juice in the morning and in the noon, and have their usual meal before Sunset; or, they should have their usual meal in the morning and take no cooked food in the evening, and take juice of fruits mixed with water, only. By gradual practice, they should learn to fast one day in the week without taking any solid food.

Fasts for over a week not only cleanse the body, but give us more energy and power and also spiritual strength. Therefore, the Sastras have praised the merits of observing Navaratri of Sri Rama, Krishna, Durga, Siva, etc.

If middle-class people observe these partial or half fasts on fruit-juice only, they will save much of their troubles and doctors' bills. Tea and coffee should be avoided not only on fasting days, but even after the fast, if possible.

## ANTIDOTES FOR INDIGESTION

1. If indigestion is caused by eating cocoanuts, taking a small quantity of rice will cure it.

2. Indigestion arising from eating mangoes is cured by drinking milk.

3. Indigestion caused by the excessive use of ghee is destroyed by the use of lemon-juice.

4. Indigestion due to eating plantains is curable by the use of *Sambhar* salt.

5. Indigestion due to eating *kali-dal* is cured by taking a little quantity of sugar.

6. Indigestion from eating cakes is cured by the use of hot water.

# HEALTH AND THE ELEMENTS

7. Indigestion from taking milk is destroyed by the use of thin curdled milk.

8. Indigestion due to drinking water is cured by taking a little honey.

9. Indigestion caused by taking apricots is destroyed by taking water freely.

10. Indigestion due to Jack fruits is curable by plantains.

## HEALTH AND THE ELEMENTS

*Composition of the Human Body:* This body is composed of the five elements—(1) Earth; (2) Water; (3) Light; (4) Air and (5) Space (Akasa). It has a natural power to heal itself. If we help this power by means of the above five elements, the work of healing is accelerated. It has a power to assimilate those things which are congenial to it and throw away matter which is foreign to it.

If a thorn enters the foot or an insect enters the eye, the body tries to drive it out; but this being a natural process, it takes time. It is our duty to aid the body in such a way as to help it in its natural process of self-cure.

*Earth* contains magnetic currents and many properties of curing diseases. It can be used in the form of hot or cold mud packs or plasters. It takes out poisons from the body and cools the system quickly. Ancient people were using earth for cleansing their bodies and hair, and many use earth in the form of Bhasma. Many Sadhus smear their bodies with Bhasma, which protects their skin from heat and cold.

*Air:* Air can be utilised in many ways in keeping the body fit. (1) We must accustom ourselves to use as few clothes as possible. (2) We must expose our body to the fresh air as much as possible. (3) We can take a walk in the morning and evening. In working hours we should try to get as much fresh air as possible by keeping the doors and windows open. (4) Running is also a good exercise for young persons. (5) We can have deep breathing. (6) We should do Surya Namaskaras or any kind of exercise, which naturally makes us inhale more air.

*Water:* Water is utilised in curing diseases in various ways.

(1) In the form of cold, hot, steam, vapour treatments; and hip, sitz, and other mineral and herbal baths, by putting those minerals and herbs in the water. Water can be used in cleansing the stomach in the form of Dhauti or "stomach wash" through a rubber tube. It can be taken as Usha-Pani or a cup of hot water instead of tea, before meals and at bedtime. Water treatment can be applied in the form of packs, cold or hot, moist or by enema. Just as water cools the engine of a motor and controls heat, so also water controls the heat of our body, and helps to expel many impurities through the skin.

*Light:* Sunlight costs nothing. So it can be utilised to its full extent. We should expose our bodies to the morning Sun and get Vitamin D from it. Rickets can be cured by Sunlight. Chromopathy can cure many diseases.

Electric light can cure some diseases; but it is somewhat costly and not free to all.

In ancient times living was most natural; now owing to the advance of science, the age of machinery has made living most artificial. Even in this age we should make use of these five elements in keeping the body as fit as possible.

*Food:* This age of machinery has multiplied luxuries, but has made articles of food most dear. The chief fuel for keeping the human machine in order is food, and now it is being found dearer and dearer.

All comforts are useless if the body is not in order. Without proper food, the body cannot remain in good health. If the body is sick, one cannot enjoy comforts.

Of all the kinds of food, fruits and milk help much to repair our body-machine. But now they are not within the reach of the poor and even of middle-class people.

Tea and coffee have taken the place of milk; but neither of them is as efficient as milk, curd, butter and buttermilk.

If a man wants real happiness, he will have to return to nature as far as practicable and be content with natural beauty and not depend upon artificial make-up.

With all the precautions, a motorist cannot avoid an accident, which may impair his machine. So this human body may become sick through some causes which are beyond our control, with all our necessary precautions.

Under these circumstances, we should try to repair the body with natural means and food remedies and fasts.

The main disease from which most of the diseases arise is constipation and indigestion. If the digestion is impaired, the whole power which keeps the body-machine in order is impaired and as other organs are overworked, various other diseases arise.

Our first duty is to have a good digestion and to keep the bowels clear by means of occasional fasts and enemas or herbal laxatives; and, in case of any disease, live on fruits and milk for a week or two, considering these as nature's remedies to drive away disease, and to regain the lost health.

## SUNLIGHT AND HEALTH

1. Today Sunlight has been scientifically studied, its properties have been investigated and its effects tabulated, and its use has been standardised. It stands now as one of the foremost agencies in the prevention and treatment of diseases.

2. Sunlight is the best masseur. It heals diseased bones, builds up weakened muscles, clears up infected tissues, and restores crippled bodies to health. The Sun treatment (Helio therapy) must be continued for months.

3. The Sun is the source of life. A Hindu worships the Sun as a God. For the ancient Aryans, Egyptians, Greeks and Romans, the Sun was the source of life. They also adored the Sun as a God.

4. The Sun is a great nutritional factor. He is also called "Pushan" in the Isavasya Upanishad. Sunlight is an essential factor for maintaining health.

5. Sunlight is a food. You can make vitamin D by exposing your naked body to the Sun. The skin and nerves will absorb the energies of Sunlight. The Sunlight provides sufficient heat that may be needed to sustain life.

6. Sunlight induces the production of vitamin D and E by its action on the skin. Sunlight cannot manufacture Vitamin A by its

action on the skin, but it produces some changes by which the least amounts of vitamin can maintain growth and health.

7. Sunlight is the great vital stimulant and preserver. Sunshine is just as necessary for animal and human life as for plant life.

8. Ultra-violet rays are short chemical rays. They have powerful effects upon living tissues. They kill the germs on the surface, increasing resistance to infection, improve the function of glands, stimulate the circulation of blood. They convert a substance in the skin known as ergosterol into vitamin D.

9. The ultra-violet rays increase calcium and phosphorus, affect the constituents of the blood, promptly cure certain bone-diseases such as rickets, increase the alkalinity of the blood and so remove acidosis, increase the iron content and blood, and are also useful in anaemia. They increase the formation of antibodies which fight infection and so build up body resistance to disease.

10. The ultra-violet rays cure certain skin diseases as ringworm, cane, boils, etc. They stimulate the healing of wounds and aid the union of fractured bones. The rays are absorbed into the blood stream. They alter the composition of the blood and influence the general health.

11. Infra-red rays are the long heat waves of Sunlight. They produce heating of the tissues and bring more blood to the parts on which they impinge and aid the absorption of the ultra-violet rays in the Sunlight.

12. Ultra-violet rays should not be confused with the violet rays, which are a form of electric current.

13. Ultra-violet rays prevent the developing of ricket. Expose your body to the ultra-violet rays of the Sun in the morning and attain good health and vigour.

14. Sun-bath is highly beneficial. Expose your body to the rays of the Sun, for a short time. Lie down on the ground on a blanket or lie on a cot. Expose your back to the rays of the Sun. If the rays are very hot, cover the back with a green plantain leaf. Remain thus for fifteen or thirty minutes till you perspire freely.

# SUNLIGHT AND HEALTH 25

This will prove useful in lumbago and rheumatism and diseases of the skin.

15. Expose the body to the morning or evening Sun for ten minutes. If you want to take a Sun-bath at 11 a.m., lie down; cover the body with a thin wet cloth or plantain leaf. Cover your head also with a plantain leaf or any green leaf or a piece of folded wet cloth. The bath may last for 10 to 20 or 30 minutes. After you get up from the bath, wipe the body with a dry clean cloth.

16. Bask in the Sun. Have a good Sun-bath in the early morning and evening. Allow the ultra-violet rays to pass through the skin. Absorb vitamin D into the system and enjoy good health.

17. The action of the Sun on the skin is due to light rays and not to heat. Therefore avoid the hot rays of the Sun and avail yourself of His cold rays.

18. The best time for having exposure to the Sun is the morning. Too much exposure to the Sun should be avoided.

19. The rays of the Sun possess the best and potent antiseptic and germicidal properties. Expose your clothing to the Sun daily and your blankets, bed-sheets, pillows and mattresses once in a fortnight.

20. Injurious germs on the skin are rendered harmless by Sunlight. Those who take Sun-bath are free from parasitic skin diseases. They are endowed with great power of endurance and resistance.

21. Sunlight produces pigmentation on the skin, which increases the capacity of absorption of the ultra-violet rays of the Sun.

22. Children need plenty of Sunlight everyday so that they may grow into healthy and robust boys or girls. If you do not have enough light, growth is interfered with and the blood becomes pale. You get anaemia or poverty of blood.

23. The Sun is the great steriliser and life-giver. You cannot have good health and nutrition without the appropriate dose of Sunlight to your skin.

24. The rays of the Sun are absolutely essential to the health of every human being.

25. Let the Sun's rays fall on the closed eyes for two or three minutes every day. This will improve your eyesight.

26. In the rays of the Sun you will find a cheap and an easily available tonic, a disinfectant, and an antiseptic and a potent germicide.

27. The skin readily absorbs Sunlight. The rays of the Sun get filtered down through the skin to the layers beneath.

28. The Sun's rays cause many changes which are beneficial to the growth and well-being of the individual.

29. Sunlight is a healer of leprosy and various other skin diseases. If plenty of light falls on the skin, there is good blood circulation.

30. Loose clothing of white fabrics allows freely permeation of the Sun's rays into the skin. Therefore wear loose clothing of white fabrics.

31. The ground glass, of which some windows are made, exclude the important ultra-violet rays. Therefore remove this.

32. Lamps are manufactured which produce artificial infra-red rays, and they are extremely useful in healing painful inflammatory conditions.

33. Thick clothing shuts the Sun's rays from the skin. Use as little clothing as possible. This is hygienic and healthy.

34. Do not shut yourself up in dark rooms. Let in every ray of Sunshine possible. You will enjoy good health.

35. Dark places where Sunlight does not penetrate breed consumption, rickets, etc. Therefore live in well-ventilated rooms where Sunlight penetrates freely.

36. Modern civilisation has forced man from his natural outdoor environments to a life within closed dark rooms that shut out the warm, life-giving beams of the Sun. He sits behind glass-windows and doors that filter out the most beneficial rays. On account of the shut-in, Sunless life he has lost his vim, vigour, vitality and health. O Man! take Sun-bath and regain your lost health and vitality.

## BATH

1. Four of the most convenient baths are: (1) Shower bath, which is in the form of a cold spray; (2) Plunge or cold dip, which is to immerse the body in cold water and then come out immediately to dry; (3) Splash bath—cold water is splashed on the body; (4) cold sponge, which consists of dipping a towel or sponge in cold water and wringing it slightly and quickly going over the body with it.

2. A bath daily in cold water in the early morning before Sunrise is really bracing, invigorating, energising and refreshing.

3. Those who can enjoy the cold bath should certainly take it every day. It is one of the best health measures that exist. It stimulates all the functions of the body and makes the skin much more resistant to cold. The effect of a cold bath is to drive the blood suddenly from the skin to the interior of the body.

4. Take cold bath. Rub the body vigorously with a towel. This is an excellent tonic to invigorate the body and strengthen it. Cold and other diseases will not be contracted easily.

5. The best time for a bath is early morning before Sunrise, because the water that gets cooled during the night evolves much oxygen at this time.

6. Do not take a cold bath immediately after performing "Asanas" or any kind of exercises. Allow the body to cool down. Wait for an hour. Never bathe soon after your meals, as it will interfere with your digestion.

## SLEEP

1. Sleep is a physiological phenomenon by which the mind, the brain and all the organs get rest for some hours. During sleep the mind goes back to its source.

2. Sleep is nature's tonic for a healthy life. The more sound sleep one has, the more healthy one would be.

3. There should be six hours sleep for a man, seven for a woman and eight for a fool. Ten hours sleep is necessary for a child.

4. Keep the same time, daily, for sleep. Wear loose clothing. Do not cover yourself with heavy blankets or clothing.

5. Never sleep on the back, but sleep on the left-side. This will not affect the heart as many ignorant people think. Allow the Surya Nadi or right nostril to flow during sleep. Food will be digested well, as Surya Nadi is heating.

6. Sleep on the sides, especially on the left-side. This helps to empty the stomach and allow the Surya Nadi or Pingala to flow.

7. Napolean Bonaparte believed in only four hours sleep. Too much sleep makes a man dull and lethargic.

8. Do not sleep in rooms which have no windows.

## PRACTICAL AIDS TO SOUND SLEEP

1. Give up the worrying habit. Worry slowly undermines the vital force. He who worries cannot sleep. Rely in God. Take refuge in Him, His name and grace. Be regular in your prayer and meditation. The worrying habit will vanish. You will have good, refreshing sleep.

2. Be cheerful. Smile always. Do Kirtan. Sing the Lord's praise. All worries will take to their heels. You will sleep well.

3. Use light bed-clothes. Do not cover yourself with too many blankets. Heavy blankets will disturb your sleep.

4. Do not take any drugs to induce sleep. A drug habit will be formed. Thirty drops of opium may give you a little sleep on the first day. Even half a bottle will not produce even a bit of sleep after some days. Drugs produce depression. Try to get sleep by natural methods.

5. Give up overloading the stomach. Let your diet be light and easily digestible. Indigestion is another cause for sleeplessness. Finish your evening meal at 5 p.m. Let it be some milk and fruits only. Do not take anything at night. You will have good sleep.

6. Relax your body and mind completely. Sleep is bound to come to you.

## PRACTICAL AIDS TO SOUND SLEEP

7. Give up heated debates and unnecessary arguments and discussions. Keep your temper under control.

8. Abandon tea and coffee entirely. They unnecessarily stimulate the cells of the brain and the nerves.

9. Do not read novels, ghost stories, thrillers, murder yarns and other sensational literature. They will excite your nerves.

10. Do not take stimulants of any kind. Give up liquors, Ganjah, opium, etc.

11. Do not do any intense brain work before retiring to bed.

12. Avoid mental flurry or agitation. Try to remain calm always. Control the emotions. Control anger.

13. Do not take exciting foodstuffs, hot curries, chutneys, too much chillies, tamarind. Let your food be bland and quite simple. Take more of milk and fruits.

14. Take oil bath just before retiring to bed or hot mustard foot bath.

15. If you wake up, do not bother to find out what the time is. To look at the watch will be to make you anxious.

16. Do not keep any light in the room. If you cannot sleep without light, then use a green chimney.

17. Apply a little Brahmi-amla oil on the head just before retiring to bed.

18. Take a cup of hot Horlick's malted milk just before retiring to bed.

19. Do a little Japa, prayer and meditation just before going to bed. Study some elevating sacred books like the Gita, the Yoga Vasishtha, the Upanishads, the Bhagavata, the Koran, the Bible, etc.

20. Give this suggestion to the mind: "O mind! You have done everything. You have obtained everything. You have got everything. Do not worry about anything. You have nothing more to do or get. Be at perfect ease. Meditate. This world is unreal. It is full of pains". This will give you perfect, restful sleep and free the mind of all worries.

21. Reduce your wants. Annihilate all desires and cravings.

Talk a little. Do not mix much. Do not fatigue yourself through overwork. Sleep alone. Have a brisk walk in the evening.

22. Develop your will. Cultivate self-control. You can sleep at your will, like Napoleon and Gandhiji, at any time, at any place, and get up at any time you like.

23. If your nerves and brain are weak, strengthen and energise them through the practice of mild Pranayama with OM Japa. Take a beverage made up of almonds, Brahmi leaves, sugar-candy and powdered black-pepper in the early morning. Take Brahmi-ghrita (ghee) or Huxley's Nervigour Syrup.

24. Take a dose of Sanatogen at night just before retiring to bed. You will have good sleep. You can take another dose in the early morning. Take it with milk.

25. Lie down quietly, relaxed in mind and body. This will give you as much recuperation as sleep itself. A little silent meditation also will give you perfect rest.

26. Put two teaspoonfuls of mustard powder in the basin of hot water. Sit on a chair or stool. Keep the legs in the water for 15 or 20 minutes. Then take the feet out of the water. Wipe them with a dry towel and put on stockings. This will give you sound sleep. This is useful in headache, vertigo, rheumatism, fever, etc. This is used for the feet to check colds.

## Chapter III

### DIET AND HEALTH

1. The diet of modern civilised races is too concentrated and too rich in protein and sugar. Therefore the intestine does not contain enough waste matter to stimulate it into action. In a natural diet containing a good proportion of whole-meal bread, fresh fruits and vegetables, this difficulty is removed.

2. Your body is continuously growing till you reach the age of 25 years. After that the build-up of body is complete. You are in need of more nutritious food during this period.

3. Your food must contain proteins or tissue-building nitrogenous substances, fats, carbohydrates and minerals in proper quantity. The life-giving substances—vitamins A, B, C, D, E, etc.,—must also be there. Their presence in due proportion is called balancing.

4. It is a mistaken theory that, if you eat more, you will put on more flesh and health. Statistics have conclusively proved that more people die annually of over-eating than under-eating.

5. Stunted growth is due to various reasons—the chief being malnutrition, want of proper exercise and poor health. Watch your diet properly and see that you get enough of all the vitamins necessary to build your flesh and bones.

6. Even people of means have children who look puny, because they are undernourished and show that they do not eat a balanced diet.

7. Children should have plenty of milk, fresh fruits and vegetables, to help their rapid growth.

8. Your diet must contain vitamins, the accessory food factors, in addition to proteins, carbohydrates, fats, salts and water, if you wish to maintain good health. Milk, cereals, potatoes, fresh leafy vegetables, juicy fruits and honey must find a place in your daily diet schedule.

9. Never eat unless you are really hungry. Beware of false hunger. Don't force yourself to eat, simply because it happens to be meal-time. If you have no appetite, it is a sure sign that the body does not need any food at that moment.

10. Do not be a slave to any diet theory. Use your commonsense. Eat things you like, and you will feel happy. Do not overstuff yourself. Chew the food well.

11. Do not be fussy or faddy. This especially applies to diet. Do not be too rigid.

12. There are no teeth in the stomach. Grinding of the food should be done by the teeth. You should not tax the stomach with work which it is not meant to do. If you do so, you commit a serious crime. You will be punished by nature with digestive disorders.

13. Do not swallow the food quickly. Masticate it slowly and thoroughly. This will give rest to the stomach and intestines.

14. Digestion starts in the mouth, where the food is subjected to the action of saliva and the physical action of mastication. Many people are used to washing down each mouthful of food with water. This is a very bad habit. Moisten the food with saliva in the mouth but not with water.

15. Eat only when you are hungry. Eat slowly. Drink plenty of water after finishing the food. Do not drink water before meals as it will dilute the gastric juice and will cause indigestion and other stomach complaints.

16. Almost all your ailments have their origin in the digestive system. Masticate well; regulate your diet; take simple, wholesome food, at the proper hours. Be regular in your exercise. Live in the open air. You will have wonderful health and vitality.

17. Have fixed time for taking food, whether twice or thrice a day.

18. Do not eat late at night and go to bed immediately after.

19. The evening meal should be light and eaten not later than 7 p.m. as a general rule.

20. Digestion takes place at night; consequently you should

take a light meal at night. Strong coffee or tea should not be taken at night.

21. Light diet consists of no solids: only milk, soda and milk, barley water, whey, cocoa, etc.

22. Next to exercise and fresh air, diet plays the chief part in the body-building programme.

23. A glass of cold water or tepid water on getting up is very good if taken regularly.

24. At the present time, there is growing concern about the relation of health and diet. Your diet must be of the proper quality. It must be a well-balanced diet. There must be variety also. Then alone will you enjoy good health and happiness.

25. Variety in food is necessary, but too many different kinds at one time are not good.

26. Raw foods are better than cooked ones. The former are more vitalising than the latter.

27. Cooking destroys the disease-producing germs and makes the food easily digestible.

28. Fried food injures the digestive organs, as it cannot be digested easily.

29. The clear liquid left after curd or cheese has been separated is called whey. It contains water, proteins, fat, carbohydrates and salt. This is very good for invalids. It is more easily digested by a weak stomach. It is most beneficial in the treatment of constipation and in diseases of the stomach and the intestinal canal.

30. Curd and water thoroughly mixed give the mixture white milky appearance, due to suspension of casein in water. It is known as Lassi in Hindi and Ghol in Bengali. This is cooling. It cleanses the blood. It is beneficial in dysentery and consumption.

31. Cheese has high nutritive value. Whey is an important supplement to many Indian diets, as it will add considerably to the nutritious value of a diet consisting of cereal products.

32. Dalia is broken wheat. It is boiled in water. Milk is added and salt or sugar is also added according to patient's taste. This is very nourishing and beneficial.

33. The first food given to many is vegetarian in character. It is not meat juice or beef tea. This indicates that vegetarian food is the natural food of man.

34. It is entirely incorrect to think that animal food is an essential article of man's dietary. There are vegetable foods which are both cheaper than meat and much cleaner and more nourishing.

35. Eminent doctors have proved that meat is the most favourable food for the development of putrefactive germs in the intestinal canal.

36. Many die of diseases due to meat-eating. Give up meat-eating and have a healthy kidney, liver and bowels.

37. Meat-eating and a high protein diet reduce one's power of endurance. Therefore abandon meat. Take a well-balanced diet.

38. Spices and condiments cater to your unnatural cravings. If your sense of taste is natural and not perverted, you not only find them unnecessary but do not relish them.

39. Condiments, tea, coffee, alcohol, foods that are rich in starch, sugars and fats and all stimulating drinks should be avoided.

40. The vegetarian diet is the most perfect diet that one can follow.

41. The intellect is rendered keen, subtle and sharp by a vegetarian diet.

42. Vegetarians should include some raw leaves in their diet. Raw leaves should be sliced and mixed with lemon-juice and salt.

43. You can conquer sleep if you live on a fruit diet alone.

44. If you take a tablespoonful of honey in hot water when you are tired or exhausted by over-exertion, it will brace you up immediately. You will become strong and active again.

45. Diabetic patients can take honey with advantage.

46. Honey kills bacteria and thus enables the body to overcome disease.

47. Honey is first class food. It is a laxative. It is a tonic and a natural rejuvenator. It is a great restorative after serious illness. Honey taken with milk-cream or butter increases the general health vigour and vitality.

48. A daily attempt at evacuation of the bowels should be made at a fixed hour. Regular exercise must be taken. Add laxative vegetable foods to the diet.

49. He who drinks buttermilk, eats tomatoes and lemons, walks three miles daily, is healthy and attains longevity.

## FRUITS AND HEALTH

1. Every kind of fruit contains valuable vitamins and minerals—elements essential for health and growth.

2. Beans, tomatoes, potatoes, radish, carrot, ladies-fingers, cucumbers, drum sticks, spinach, green leafy vegetables are all pure, delicious and nutritious foods and can be taken with much advantage.

3. Dried fruits, raisins, dates and figs are valuable foods with a high nutritive content. Nuts are among the most nutritive of all foods.

4. Tomatoes, carrots, lemons, a little ginger, a little coriander leaves, a little fresh ginger and curd form a very good healthy combination. This is a good appetiser.

5. *Bananas:* Banana or plantain fruit contains A, B, C and D vitamins. This is a very good soothing food. You can live on milk and bananas alone. They are very nutritious. They promote growth, augment vigour and add flesh to the body. The fully ripe fruits act as a laxative. Take one or two fruits at bed time. You will have free movement of the bowels in the morning.

6. *Carrots:* Carrots beautify the skin. They improve the blood and the appetite. Take it raw. Carrot halwa is a brain tonic.

7. *Lemon:* Lemon contains salts and a large amount of Vitamin C, which is necessary for general good health. It acts against scurvy. It is an anti-scorbutic. It stops bleeding from the gums. Take the juice of one fruit with 2 table-spoonfuls of honey as the first thing in the morning.

8. *Mangoes:* Mangoes contain sugar and highly refined turpentine in them. They also contain iron and other useful acids. They are useful in rheumatism, diarrhoea and diabetes.

9. *Oranges:* Orange juice mixed with fresh grape juice makes a very good tonic. This is very useful in anaemia or poverty of blood, general debility, rickets, etc.

10. *Papaya:* Papaya contains the active principle of alkaloid papain. The latter digests the food rapidly.

11. *Pineapple:* Pineapple is very beneficial in case of enlargement of spleen. Take one fruit daily.

12. *Potatoes:* Potatoes supply the body with potash and salts.

13. *Spinach:* Spinach (palak) is a healthy, wholesome green vegetable. It is a kind of leaf. It contains iron. Spinach and tomatoes will improve the blood qualitatively and quantitatively. Tomatoes also contain a lot of iron.

14. *Tomatoes:* Tomato was first discovered in South America, whence it was introduced into Europe during the sixteenth century. People held the notion that tomatoes were poisonous.

15. Tomatoes stimulate the action of the liver and contain all the vitamins.

16. Tomato is a powerful de-obstruent, i.e., remover of disease particles and opener of the natural channels of the body. It is one of the most wonderful and effective blood-cleansers known to man.

17. Tomatoes contain the salt, potash, lime, magnesia and iron. They exercise a beneficial effect on the liver, kidneys and other organs.

18. They cure also constipation.

19. Tomatoes contain citric acid and a small quantity of oxalic acid. It contains large quantities of five of the six vitamins. Cooking partially destroys their vitamin content. Therefore, tomatoes should be eaten raw.

## MILK AND HEALTH

1. Milk is a balanced food. It contains all the nutritive principles in a well-balanced proportion. It is highly recommended not only for children but for adults also.

2. Milk has all the energy-giving nutrients, all the known vitamins and all important mineral elements. These exist in a form that admits of easy digestion and assimilation.

3. The nutritive value of milk lies in its promotion of growth and in the protection it affords against disease. It is the food provided by nature when new tissues are being formed.

4. As milk contains all the materials essential for growth and maintenance of life in a form ready for utilisation by the body, it is obviously of high value.

5. Milk is ideal medium for the growth of pathogenic or disease-causing germs. All milk in the tropics should as a rule be boiled.

6. Always boil the milk before drinking. Boiled milk is free from tubercle bacilli and other germs. After boiling the milk, do not allow it to stand more than 5 hours before drinking; for disease-germs grow very rapidly in milk.

7. As milk is growth-promoting, children and adolescents, expectant and nursing mothers need it in large quantities than others.

8. A diet of milk alone is not desirable for children, adolescents, adults. Since relatively to its bulk it is deficient in energy-giving constituents, it needs to be supplemented with iron, vitamin D and vitamin C in the form of orange juice, etc.

9. From one or two pints a day is desirable for children, about 2 pints a day for nursing and expectant mothers. A minimum of half-pint is desirable for the adult under ordinary conditions in order to secure a sufficiency of calcium and also good quantity of protein.

10. Investigations have definitely shown that milk is an essential element in the diet of children to secure optimum growth or physique and for the maintenance of health.

11. Investigations have also shown that milk is all-important for the development of normal teeth resistance to dental caries.

12. It is very important to increase the milk supply in order to improve the general health of a community. It will secure better bone formation and improve physique, diminish the incidence of disease, particularly rickets, and increase resistance to dental caries.

13. Every effort to improve the dairying industry is a nation-building activity.

## BETWEEN MEAT AND MILK

**Place:** A dairy product stall in the New Market in Calcutta. In the hall are laid several tables and four chairs around each. At one corner is the "Milk Bar", where two well-dressed attendants are issuing milk bottles to the customers. To the right is another stall, and another attendant leans over it, cutting flesh, weighing it on the balance and handing it to customers across the counter.

'Tup'! Opens a milk bottle and the cork flies! The attendants are astounded and sink into their chairs. Again, the flaps of the packets containing sliced mutton, too, open out with a peculiar noise. The attendants duck behind the counters, and with eyes on a level with the counter-bar watch the following scene.

*Meat:* (To milk) O Milk! what a horrible distinction they make between us! They have given three attendants to be in charge of milk distribution here: whereas I am allotted only one ......

*Milk:* (Laughing) Yes, yes, and rightly indeed! The Prime Minister has an army of peons, whereas a Chotah officer has one, and that, too, he has to share with another (Laughs aloud).

*Meat:* O Milk! I am superior to you. (Emphatically) I contain the protein serum albumin in me, 5.97 in a gramme. Your protein lactalbumin is only .94 in a gramme.

*Milk:* Mere percentage of protein cannot make you superior to me. What is the use of mere bulk? Your protein is like black sugar or *gud*. My protein is like refined sugar. It is concentrated essence like saccharin. It is more powerful.

*Meat:* (Angrily) I sit on the tables of great Barons and Lords in the West......

*Milk:* (Lightly) Pooh, I sit before the Rishis, seers and Yogis of India. I am adored in Yajnas. I purify the heart of men. I am one of the ingredients of Pancha Gavya. I am Sattvic. You are Rajasic.

*Meat:* I infuse a new spirit into the Generals and soldiers in the war.

*Milk:* This is, indeed, a wrong notion. This is an old false belief of beer drinkers. It only produces excitement. Real, great Generals are all my votaries. They take milk sop.

*Meat:* My followers are abundant in the world. I am respected everywhere.

*Milk:* Satan has great followers in this world? (Laughs loudly).

*Meat:* (In great rage) Fie on thee, you call me a Satan......?

*Milk:* Something more than Satan. Even good scientists and poets are leaving you now. They have come to my side.

*Meat:* I.....help people in thinking.

*Milk:* This is also an erroneous idea. Pythagoras, Plato, Aristotle, Socrates, were all vegetarians. So were G.B. Shaw, Sir Stafford Cripps; so was Mahatma Gandhiji. Meat is unhygienic, dangerous and unnatural. It is unnecessary. It produces tapeworms and various kinds of diseases of worms. It produces gout and rheumatism.

*Meat:* I am more nutritious than you. Doctors recommend to patients meat juice, meat broths and meat soup.

*Milk:* Certainly not. I am the food for the invalids, convalescent and babies. Only Asuric doctors of bygone days used to recommend meat juice, etc. Many modern sensible doctors are against meat. Go through the reports of Dr. Josiah Oldfield, Dr. Sir Henry Thomson., M.D., F.R.C.S., you will know the truth of my statement.

*Meat:* In the restaurants of Europe, hotel-keepers make several preparations of me. They surely like me more...

*Milk:* You have not visited Bengal and U.P. Halwais have a thousand and one preparations of me. You will be stunned. Come and visit once. There are Rubbadis, Pedas, Sandesh, Rasagullas, Kalakand, etc. The names themselves of these preparations are charming. They excite the nerves of taste of people. All Europeans in Bengal fill their stomach with Rasagullas and Sandesh.

*Meat:* Thank you, my friend Milk! Let us shake hands now. I am defeated. I am your intimate friend now. I will not quarrel with you. I have lost my suzerainty. At least give me some pension in my old age, as I served people in olden days. Let not my name be blotted out entirely. Let me be remembered like Ravana of yore. Namaste!

> [The cork resumes its position on the milk-bottle. The lids of the meat-packet close up. The amazed waiters raise their heads and make sure that the conversation is over.]

*Waiter No. 1:* Manager Saheb! Did you hear.....

*Manager:* Yes, Ghulam, I did hear the wonderful conversation. From this afternoon there will be no sale of meat in our stall. Put up a board to that effect outside. Arrange for more milk and for sweets also.

*Waiter No. 1:* Yes Saheb!

(Curtain Drops)

## HEALTH, HYGIENE AND DIET

This body is temple of God.
The Lord is the Proprietor of this temple,
He is the Indweller.
It is an instrument for God-realisation.
Therefore it should be kept healthy and strong.
It is a wonderful engine.
The digestion of food, the pumping of blood,
The secretion and excretion,
The functions of brain, liver, heart,
Kidneys and lungs are marvellous.

Food supplies materials
For growth, maintenance and repair,
Food supplies energy to heart
The Proteins are the tissue-builders,
The Prana builds the tissues,
Vitamins are the life-giving substances,
Carbohydrates and fats generate energy,
Minerals are body-building materials.

## HEALTH MENU

Have a restricted diet on Sunday
Take on all-fruit diet on Monday
Live on full milk diet on Tuesday
Have the fruit and milk diet on Wednesday
Have full fast on Thursday, the Guru's day
Take all-vegetable diet on Friday
Have partial fast on Saturday,
Take milk and fruits only at night.
If you stick to the above dietetic regimen,
Diseases will take to their heels,
You will possess good health and strength,
You will attain longevity,
This will aid you in attaining concentration,
You will have very good meditation.
Try this, follow this and realise the results.

## SHUN ONION PAKKODA

Onion Pakkoda contains onions, chillies, a little of ginger, Bengal-gram flour and sweet neem leaves and coriander leaves and salt. This is a palatable preparation which pleases the palate but takes the man away from God, as the mind ever thinks of Pakkoda but not of God.

If you peel the onion layer after layer, it dwindles into nothing. Even so, if you peel this ego layer after layer, it dwindles into airy nothing.

Onion has medicinal properties. It is useful in cholera. A few onions are crushed and the juice is given to the cholera patient. It acts as a specific. It is endowed with germicidal properties. It kills the cholera germs at once. Onion contains sulphur, and so it is useful to those who suffer from piles or haemorrhoids.

But it is a deadly poison for a religious aspirant. It is worse than meat. It excites the passion, fills the mind with Rajas and destroys serenity of mind. You cannot have good concentration. So is garlic or lahsoon. Aspirants and householders who tread the path of truth should shun it as a virulent poison.

Even some of learned Pundits take onion Pakkoda voraciously and argue that the onions possess medicinal properties and are good for maintaining good health. They support their argument by saying that Mahatma Gandhiji also took onions occasionally and recommended onions for his Ashramites and others. Gandhiji may have recommended onions for medicinal purposes. He would not have recommended onions for those who tread the path of spirituality. This is only their trick and crookedness to take onions. Gandhiji never took onions.

Some Sannyasins and aspirants take onion Pakkoda. They say "we take under medical grounds and for health. We are above 'good and evil'. We have equal vision. Onion and milk appear same in our eyes". This is quite absurd. This is Asuric philosophy. They also come under the category of the above mentioned Pundits. Sannyasins and aspirants should lead an exemplary life. Even if a man drinks milk underneath a palmyra tree, people will say that he took toddy only. There are certainly so many other medicines and herbs than onion Pakkoda.

Even orthodox Pundits make their children eat plenty of onion Pakkodas. They think that their children will be strong and healthy by taking these 'tonic-pakkodas'. This is bad training. This is a serious error. Bad food leads to bad character. Bad exciting food exercises a tremendous evil influence on the mind.

Parents should give Sattvic food to their children even from their boyhood, and help them in cultivating good character. Those who give onion Pakkodas to their children are culprits. They are responsible for the bad traits of their children. They have failed in their duty of bringing up their children in the path of righteousness.

May you all refrain from taking onion Pakkodas and giving

# SHUN ONION PAKKODA

onion Pakkodas to your children. May you feed the children with Sattvic food and bring them up in the path of divinity! May you all take Sattvic food and thus attain everlasting peace!

# Chapter IV

## DISCOVERY OF VITAMINS

There are some mysterious substances in food in very minute quantities. They are indispensable for the nutrition of the body. Their chemical composition is not yet known, but it is known that serious diseases result when they are absent or deficient. These mysterious substances are called vitamins.

Vitamins were first discovered by Sir Frederic Gowland Hopkins, the English Food Scientist in 1912. They are chemical substances found in all natural foodstuffs. The vitamins play a vital part in maintaining and regulating the health of the organism.

Previously it was customary, when considering the question of food, to take into account only five factors, which are known as "The Proximal Principles". It was believed that the food which contained all these factors in a certain proportion was the right kind of food and could properly maintain the health of men and animals. These five factors are proteins, carbohydrates, fats, minerals and water. It was Hopkins who proved conclusively by experiments that certain "accessory food factors" are essential for the maintenance of health, for growth, stamina, physical efficiency and nutrition. These accessory food factors are the mysterious Vitamins.

Experiments were made on rats. The well-fed rats remained free from disease. The ill-fed rats showed morbid states both clinically and at post-mortem examination. Diseases of the eye, actual blindness, diseases of the skin, neuritis, Beri-beri, scurvy, decay of teeth, rickets or softening of the bones, were present in the ill-fed rats. This indicates that mankind in general suffers from one major disease—Malnutrition—and that many of the diseases from which it suffers arise chiefly from this cause.

The classification and definition of vitamins is made according to the effect of these vitamins on the human organism.

# DISCOVERY OF VITAMINS

The name Vitamin is derived from the Latin word 'Vita' meaning life, because vitamins are essential for life.

Actual experiments showed that animals could not live on mixture of proteins, carbohydrates, fats and mineral salts. But an addition of a small quantity of milk to the mixture of pure foods made a vast difference. Scientists began to enquire what it is in milk that exerts such a profound influence on nutrition. Investigations and experiments revealed the existence of a number of substances now known as Vitamins. They are named by the letters of the alphabet, A, B, C, D, E.

Lunin made some experiments. He kept two sets of mice. He fed one set with fresh milk alone and the other set with casein, fat, sugar and minerals in their isolated pure form. The first set grew normally, but the second set began to lose weight and died after five weeks. The experimental diet in the latter case satisfied all the physiological requirements in respect of protein, carbohydrates, fat and minerals, but had still failed to provide nourishment to the mice. Lunin thought that other substances which are indispensable for nutrition must be present in milk besides casein, milk, sugar, fat and minerals. Experiments were conducted by Prof. F.G. Hopkins. His experiments on rats were soon confirmed by other independent workers of Germany and America. The conclusion arrived at was: "Fresh milk, besides containing protein, sugar, fat and minerals, contains certain substances of unknown composition but indispensable for an all-round nutrition". These substances of unknown composition were named by Hopkins as "accessory food factors".

Later experiments revealed that the unknown substances which are essential for nutrition are present in the butter of milk and that the unknown substances are present in some forms of fats such as butter, cream, cod liver oil, etc., and absent from almond oil, coconut oil, cotton seed oil, linseed oil, etc.

The nutritive substances of unknown composition present in good fats were termed "Fat-soluble A vitamin".

Further experiments led to the discovery of Water-soluble B Vitamin, Water-soluble C Vitamin, etc.

## CLASSIFICATION OF VITAMINS

Vitamins are classified as follows: Vitamin A, Vitamin B (Vitamin B-1, Vitamin B-2), Vitamin C, Vitamin D and Vitamin E.

Vitamin A, D, E are soluble in fat and are associated with the fat of certain foods.

Vitamin B-1, B-2 and C are soluble in water and widely distributed in foods.

Scurvy used to be the scourge of the British Navy, until the introduction of lemon juice as a prophylactic. During the Great War there was abundant opportunity of studying the disease, which by then had become very rare. The research carried on at the Lister Institute by Dr. Harriette Chick and others established the fact that the anti-scorbutic vitamin is contained in large amount in fresh lemons, oranges and fresh green vegetables; in moderate amount in roots, such as swedes and potatoes; and in small amount in milk and fresh meat. It is absent in dried and preserved food. As alkalies destroy the vitamin, soda should not be used in cooking vegetables. In expeditions and long voyages, when fresh vegetables are not available, the daily ration should contain an ounce of lemon or orange juice with sugar, and some peas, beans, or lentils which have germinated. The pulses do not contain vitamins except when they have germinated. The germinating process is carried out thus. Soak the pulses in water at 60 degree F. for 24 hours: drain off the water, spread out in thin layers and keep moist for 48 hours at 60 degree F. Then cook rapidly (peas 40 to 60, lentils 20 minutes). Prolonged methods of cooking destroy the vitamins: hence, when food containing any vitamin is scarce, roasting and quick boiling is preferable to stewing and simmering.

Vitamins exist in food in such very tiny small quantities that till the beginning of this century even their existence had passed unobserved. Now they can be extracted and isolated from the things in which they are found in nature. They can actually be manufactured by chemical processes. These are known as "Synthetic Vitamins".

All vitamins originally were from the vegetable kingdom.

Those found in milk, eggs and fresh-oils are due to the green plants eaten by the animals.

Vitamins A, D, E and B-2 are stored in the body, while B-1 and C are not stored to a great extent. When there is deficiency of vitamin, it is drawn from the quantity that is stored.

All the vitamins except vitamin C are quite stable and are not easily destroyed by cooking. Vitamin C is easily destroyed in ordinary cooking temperature.

Some of the water soluble Vitamins may be lost if the water used in cooking is thrown away. The water also should be drunk. Or sufficient quantity of water only should be used for cooking. Vegetables and rice should be steamed. The addition of an alkali destroys the vitamins. So the practice of adding soda in cooking is not good. The addition of tamarind preserves the Vitamins.

As Vitamin C is destroyed by cooking, it is necessary to have fresh vegetables, fresh fruits like oranges or lemons, which contain Vitamin C.

Green leaves and growing shoots are richest in Vitamins. Fruits, roots and seed embryos come next.

## DIETETIC INSTRUCTIONS

The food should be rich in all its principles, particularly in the case of children, because their rapidly growing bodies demand them. If children are fed on food lacking in Vitamins, their vitality is impaired, and their power of resistance to infection is lowered. They become the first victims of epidemic diseases.

A nursing mother should get an abundant supply of such foods as are rich in vitamins, so that the breast milk may also be rich in vitamin. As milk does not contain a sufficient quantity of B and C vitamins, half an ounce of orange juice or tomato juice should be given daily to the children.

An adult should take a pint of milk and a child a quart.

Vegetables should be taken twice a day. Green leafy vegetables like spinach are highly beneficial.

If the diet is well balanced, if you take whole-grain cereals with milk, fresh fruits and fresh green leafy vegetables, you will get no deficiency disease.

All the Vitamin concentrates sold in the market, the synthetic products, should be carefully used and only upon the advice of a physician. Using excess of Vitamins has a bad effect. Always consult a doctor when you use these things.

Patent vitamin foods are neither necessary nor advisable. It is usually better to spend the money on fruits, vegetables, salads, milk. These foods not only supply us with Vitamins but also with other food factors which may not be present in patent foods. Even the Vitamins which are supposed to be in the patent food may not be present in sufficient amount to be of much value.

Marmite and Bemax are rich sources of Vitamin B-1.

## MYSTERIOUS VITAMINS IN FOOD

The vitamin conception has gradually evolved from the results of a number of workers pursuing the subjects in two different fields. That the substance sought in each field proved to be identical is of particular interest in strengthening the claims of the vitamin school. The recognition that certain organic substances which are present in very small quantities in certain foodstuffs play an important part in nutrition was the starting point of this enquiry. In the absence of such substances in the food, growth may be checked, and there is reason to assume that diseases such as Beri-beri, Scurvy and possibly also Rickets, result from a deficiency of these organic substances.

The scientific investigation of Beri-beri established the fact that the increase of Beri-beri coincided with the introduction of polished rice. This process of cleaning consists mainly in removing the outer coatings and giving to the rice grains a glossy surface by friction. This led to the great discovery that with the rejected outer coatings of the grains, the husks, the substances capable of preventing the disease were extracted. These bodies were named Vitamins.

*Vitamins have been called the battery of the body.* As an automobile cannot run without the battery, no matter how much gasoline is supplied, so life activities cannot continue without a supply of vitamins in the diet. A non-flesh diet is likely to supply a greater abundance of Vitamins than a flesh diet. Flesh foods are deficient in vitamins; but vitamins are supplied in abundance by milk, eggs, greens, also by other vegetables and fruits, especially raw foods, for vitamins are partially or wholly destroyed by heat.

To those who live upon a mixed diet, the loss of vitamin in one component does not generally signify, because it can be made up by other foods. The diet should include some uncooked food every day, perhaps every meal. The foods that have been refined, such as white flour, white sugar, white rice, have been robbed of their vitamins and, if eaten in any quantity, make it more difficult to secure a sufficiency of these essentials. If one uses some fresh green fruits, some milk, together with bread, one would obtain the amounts of vitamin required for growth and the actual quantitative difference from various sources. A well-balanced diet without any fads or fancies will be a perfect, hygienic diet, to supply these vitamins in proper proportions. It will not be unnecessary, of course, to reiterate, in conclusion, that these vitamins are absolutely indispensable for our life-activities, growth, structure and development.

## DIETETIC VALUE OF VITAMINS

Perhaps the most striking among recent advances in the science of nutrition is the discovery that natural foods contain substances which, while they do not belong to any previously recognised category among foodstuffs, and are in every case present in very small amounts, are yet of profound importance to the nutrition of animals and men. Their chemical nature is as yet unknown, but they are neither mystical nor intangible. They may, as definite substances, be destroyed or removed when natural foods are artificially treated. The water that is used in boiling vegetable contains a valuable supply of vitamins and, on this account, should not be thrown away. In order to preserve the vitamins, vegetables, as a rule, should not be boiled, they should be steamed with a minute quantity of water, as they themselves contain a sufficient quantity of water. In a similar manner, Siam rice, which is highly polished by a special process of milling and which possesses a specially attractive appearance which is one of its greatest claims to popularity, is deprived of this vital element vitamin by its outer covering of the seed being machined away until the hard pearl-like inner part alone remains. The outer skin removed consists very largely of an ingredient of highly chemical value in foods, known as vitamin. A person who lives upon a varied diet obtains all the vitamins he requires from other sources than rice and may, therefore, consume a moderate quantity of polished rice with impunity. On the contrary, an individual who lives on polished rice alone in the main, runs an imminent risk of developing Beri-beri.

The constituents of natural foods which go by the name of vitamins can be extracted from plants by ordinary chemical methods and this added, if not in a pure condition, yet in a concentrated form, to dietaries otherwise deficient in them.

At no time in the history of the study of metabolism (which means the constructive and destructive changes that are taking place inside the human mechanism in the economy of nature) has there been a more interesting situation than there is at present. We are apparently on the threshold of far-reaching discoveries that promise to revolutionise our conception of food-values. Not so long ago, the dietician was concerned with the nitrogenous food-stuffs, carbohydrates, fatty substances, and inorganic nutrients. It was not until recently that, in the course of investigation into the cause of Beri-beri, it was found that the disease appeared mostly in localities where polished rice was used. This led to the assumption that there were some elements in the husks of the rice that inhibited the development of the disease. It is Casimir Funk who named this element "Vitamin", and to him we should offer our sincere thanks and him we should regard as on a level with Jenner and Leister.

So far, three kinds of vitamins are known, each having qualities and functions of a special kind. The first is the anti-scorbutic vitamin that acts against scurvy, which occurs largely in sailors. If this is completely absent from the diet of any individual, scurvy rapidly results. This vitamin is soluble in water and is styled as water soluble vitamin—"Water-soluble A". The second is the anti-neuritic substance, known also as water

## DIETETIC VALUE OF VITAMINS

soluble vitamin or "Water-soluble B". In its absence, the disease Beri-beri supervenes. The third vitamin is the vitamin, "Fat-soluble A". This is soluble in fats. When it is not supplied in the foods, the result may be actual disease, but it is certain also that even a relative deficiency in any one of them may lead to malnutrition. Bony children generally suffer from rickets and are lacking in their system sufficient quantity of fat soluble vitamin. Should this be replaced, they will immediately build up their frames.

It should not be forgotten that vitamins are essential to growth, development and maintenance of normal standard of health.

Three types of vitamins are now recognised, viz., Fat-soluble A, Water-soluble B or anti-neurite vitamin, and water-soluble C or anti-scorbutic vitamin.

Fat soluble A vitamin is present in milk, butter, egg-yolk and yellow, vegetable oils, yellow corn, cream, cabbages, potatoes, beans, fat, fish, some meat, carrots, fat beef, Herring, kidney, heart, Lettuce, liver, Cod liver oil, cotton seed oil, oil Margarine (animal), Pancreas, Pea nuts, peas, fresh and dried rice, Raw fish, Spinach, wheat grain, yeast, etc. In connection with the influence of this kind of vitamin in the food, it is said to prevent rickets. The vitamin school has done an undoubted service to medicine in focussing attention on the dietetic factor in ricket, and the results obtained on animals are singularly striking. Cod liver oil stands pre-eminent in containing the largest quantity of vitamin A. Cocoanut and cocoanut oil also are very rich in Vitamin A.

Water soluble B vitamin is present in the husks of cereals, in eggs, yeast, most vegetables, some meat. This vitamin is of historical interest, since the name "vitamin" was first applied to this substance. This vitamin was isolated from rice polishings and yeast.

The anti-scorbutic vitamin or water soluble C has had a chequered career; but with a revival in the interest in Scurvy occasioned solely by its occurrence during the first world war, it has become recognised as a specific substance. Before the advent of Steamships, when voyages often extended to many months and sailors were compelled to live for long periods upon dry biscuits and salt meat, one of the most dreaded dangers of the sea was Scurvy. One day it was discovered that lime juice could prevent this terrible disease. Just why lime exercised this protective power was not known, but it was recognised that something was lacking in the ordinary food which could be supplied by this fruit juice. There is no doubt that scurvy is due to a deficiency of Vitamin C and that its treatment involves simply a control of the diet. Fresh milk contains the anti-scorbutic vitamin, but this is destroyed by sterilisation. Fresh lemon juice, the juice of cabbage and orange juice are very rich in this vitamin and are efficacious in the treatment of this deficiency disease. Experience in the war showed that fresh meat is also an important anti-scorbutic and this was well-illustrated in Mesopotamia.

## VITAMINS AND HEALTH

Vitamin means 'life-giving'. Vitamins are life-giving substances or essential food substances the presence of which is necessary for normal health. This discovery of Vitamins is comparatively recent and still in its infancy. It is a discovery of great importance. If you have some understanding of how to make use of Vitamins in the cooking and planning of your foods, you can do much to keep yourself in health and assist recovery in sickness.

It is not necessary for you to make an intensive study of the subject. Have a clear understanding of the uses of each of the known vitamins and the foods which contain them. This is more than sufficient.

In addition to the building, maintaining and working materials, some other substances in minute quantity are necessary to make the body function properly. These substances are the Vitamins. If the human system is deprived of any one of them, organs fail to rise equal to serious complications, and the absence or deficiency of these in food prevents growth of body, gives rise to certain diseases known as deficiency diseases and eventually causes death. They are present in small quantities in

# VITAMINS AND HEALTH

the foods. They are like a spark which ignites the fire of nutrition.

The nature and character of six kinds of Vitamins have been found out. The Vitamins which chiefly concern us are known as A, B, C, and D. If you have a proper supply of these vitamins in your daily diet, you should keep in good health and build up a resistance to disease.

Fresh fruits and vegetables and raw foods are richer in Vitamins.

## VITAMIN A

This promotes growth and is necessary for the proper formation of bone. It is specially important for children. It is necessary for the steady growth of children. It wards off infection from disease-causing germs. Therefore it is called Anti-infective Vitamin. It keeps the body in repair. Vitamins A and D are frequently found together in nature, especially in animal-fats. Vitamin A guards against infection, especially of the nose and the throat. In grown-up people a lack of this vitamin causes loss of weight and a tendency to suffer from colds and catarrh. Vitamin A is an essential substance for animal life. It is a fat soluble substance. Animal fats generally contain Vitamin A. Cod liver oil is very rich in Vitamin A. Leaves are the stores of vitamin A. Cocoanut oil contains a little of vitamin A.

The chief effects of Vitamin A deficiency are gradual cessation of growth, loss of weight, a decreased resistance to diseases, the development of Xeropthalmia, night-blindness, etc.

Vitamin A is contained particularly in Cod liver oil, fresh milk, butter, cream, ghee, eggs, green vegetables, green leaves.

Vitamin A is slowly destroyed by cooking. The food loses a portion of vitamin A every time it is heated.

Vitamin A gives a good tone to the skin and the mucous membrane and prevents the entry of germs through them. If there is deficiency of Vitamin A, germs easily enter through the skin and the mucous membrane.

Vitamin A cures rickets, decay of teeth, night-blindness, sore-eyes and other eye-diseases. The yellow skin of cucumber and of yellow or red chillies contains Vitamin A. All the highly coloured fruits and vegetables contain Vitamin A.

Foods rich in Vitamin A are Cod liver oil, yolk of egg, liver of animals, milk, ghee, butter, cream, green leaves such as of spinach, lettuce, cabbage, turnip, tomatoes, soya beans, green vegetables, radish tops, carrots, oranges, lemons, grapes, apples, pineapples.

Foods which contain a moderate quantity of Vitamin A are cucumber skin, maize gram, figs, watercress, runner beans.

Foods which contain a little Vitamin A are Dals, beans, wheat, rice, chillies, cocoanut oil, etc.

Foods which do not contain Vitamin A are meat, vegetable oil, polished rice, beef, potato, onion, banana, white flour.

## VITAMIN B

This is necessary for proper growth and development. This is anti-neuritic. This is the most important Vitamin for health and well-being. This is a complex water-soluble Vitamin which is divided into two parts B-1 and B-2. Absence of Vitamin B causes cessation of growth. Vitamin B-1 deficiency produces Beri-beri. Deficiency of Vitamin B-2 produces pellagra.

Vitamin B should be included in the daily diet of every child. It gives us nervous strength and vitality, helps to keep ourselves free from digestive troubles and enables us to keep that feeling of fitness so necessary if we are to enjoy our lives. Deficiency of this Vitamin leads to loss of appetite, indigestion, constipation or diarrhoea and a general breakdown of health.

Vitamin B is in the outer coating of rice and wheat. When this outer coating of rice is removed by polishing, the rice loses the Vitamin B.

Cow's milk contains enough Vitamin B. Buttermilk contains this vitamin. Butter contains little or none.

The food of mothers must be rich in Vitamin B. Then only will the babies get their quota of Vitamin B for their growth and development.

Vegetables and leaves are good sources of Vitamin A and B.

Vitamin B is not destroyed by cooking. The fluids from the

cooked rice or vegetables should not be thrown off, because they contain vitamin B.

Rice bran contains a lot of Vitamin B.

The chief sources of Vitamin B for men are the cereals. Cereals, unpolished rice, wheat, yeast, cabbage, yolk of eggs, lentils, peas, beans, nuts, turnips, potatoes, milk, oats, fruits, tomatoes, millet, pulses, spinach, carrots, green vegetables, leaves, lettuce, whole-meal bread, contain Vitamin B. Yeast is a concentrated form of Vitamin B.

## VITAMIN C

This Vitamin is called anti-scorbutic because the lack of this Vitamin produces scurvy. This vitamin has been synthesised and is known as ascorbic acid. It is an auxiliary to Vitamins A and B. It helps to maintain health generally. Vitamin C is necessary in abundant quantity to keep the blood pure and the teeth and gums and the body in good health.

It was found out that sailors used to suffer from a disease called scurvy during long voyages when they could not get fresh vegetables and fruits to eat. In this disease the gums become sore and bleed, the legs swell and begin to pain. This is prevented, or those suffering from this disease recover, if they are given the juice of lemons. This vitamin is destroyed by cooking, heating, storing and tinning. It is readily destroyed by heat in an alkaline medium (hence by sterilising milk, and boiling green vegetables with Soda). As alkalies destroy this vitamin, soda should not be used in cooking vegetables.

Tomatoes are very rich in Vitamin C. The following foods contain Vitamin C. Tangerines, apples, lemons, oranges, strawberries, gooseberries, raspberries, currants, grapefruit, cabbage, turnips, green peas, spinach, watercress, lettuce, bananas, carrots, cress, green vegetables, germinated pulses, mangoes, onions, peas, potatoes.

The research carried on at the Lister Institute established the fact that this anti-scorbutic vitamin is contained in a large proportion in fresh lemons, oranges and fresh green vegetables; in moderate amount in roots, such as swedes and potatoes; and in small amount in milk and fresh meat. It is absent in dried and preserved foods. The pulses do not contain the vitamin except when they have germinated. The germinating process is thus carried out. Soak the pulses in water at 60 degree F. for 24 hours. Drain off the water, spread out in thin layers and keep moist for 28 hours at 60 degree F. Then cook rapidly (peas 40 to 60, lentils 20 minutes). Prolonged methods of cooking destroy the vitamin. Hence, when food containing any Vitamin is scarce, roasting and quick boiling is preferable to stewing and simmering.

## VITAMIN D

Vitamin D prevents rickets, sterility and Tuberculosis. This is called anti-rachitic vitamin. This is a fat-soluble vitamin essential for the normal absorption and utilisation of calcium and phosphorus. In its absence, calcium, phosphorus are insufficiently absorbed. This vitamin has recently been synthesised as calciferol, which is derived from irradiated Ergosterol. In the human skin, calciferol is produced by ultra-violet rays. Hence the curative value of Sunlight and artificial ultra-violet waves.

The lack of this vitamin produces rickets in children in which the bones are not developed and so are weak and soft. The lack of this vitamin produces Osteomalacia in older persons. Malformation of the body is due to lack of this vitamin. Formation of bone cannot take place if calcium and phosphates are not present in due balanced condition or proper proportion. Vitamin D helps the formation of bones with the aid of calcium and phosphates. Even if calcium and phosphates are present in proper proportion, the bones cannot be formed without a proper supply of Vitamin D, the forming Agency.

Vitamin D helps us to absorb valuable minerals contained in other foods. It is essential for children and helps them to have firm muscles and good teeth.

Vitamin D is found in large quantities in Cod liver oil, in all fish oils and in herbs that have been dried in the Sun. It is very important as it makes up in some measure for the lack of Sun. Butter also contains Vitamin D. It is contained in the following foods: Salmon, Herrings, Cod liver oil, eggs, milk, butter, ghee, mushrooms, dried parsley, buttermilk, olive oil, red palm oil.

Vegetable oils develop Vitamin D when they are exposed to the Sun. The human system can synthesise vitamin D from the Sun's rays.

Children who suffer from Vitamin D deficiency cry out on the slightest handling. There is delay in dentition. They have poor teeth. Smear the body of the child with mustard oil or any oil and expose it to the Sun. This is a good method of imbibing Vitamin D.

Food must contain the bone-making mineral substances of calcium and phosphorus in proper proportion. Exposure to the Sun is of no help when these are not present in the system. It is not correct to conclude that deficiency in rickets or Osteomalacia is due only to the absence of Sunlight.

The natural method of procuring Vitamin D is to eat food containing ergosterol, which is very widely distributed in all kinds of natural foodstuffs, and then to have this activated in the skin by the ultra-violet rays of the Sun. The skin is a reservoir of light to human well-being. Anything which prevents the direct access of Sunlight to skin, such as cloudy atmosphere, clothes, indoor life, means so much loss to health and physical efficiency. Light clothing and open-air life are very conducive to health and long life.

## VITAMIN E

This is known as the anti-sterility vitamin. In its absence, degeneration of the seminiferous tubules of the male, and cessation of pregnancy with abortion in the female, occur. It is contained in wheat-germs, whole-meal bread, olive oil and greens, particularly lettuce.

He who dwells in the vitamins, who is within the vitamins, whom the vitamins do not know, whose body the vitamins are, who rules the vitamins from within is Thy Atman, Inner Ruler (Antaryamin), Amrita (Immortal).

## VITAMINS

Vitamins are necessary food-factors which are present in all natural diets of men and animals. They are body-builders. They are essentials to life. They are necessary for the maintenance of health and growth. Their absence or deficiency in food prevents growth of body, gives rise to certain diseases, known as deficiency diseases and ultimately causes death. So far five kinds of Vitamins are known. They have been classified as: A, B, C, D and E. They cannot be produced and isolated in a pure state with the exception of vitamin D.

Vitamin A (anti-infective vitamin) is fat-soluble. It promotes growth. It raises the bodily resistance against diseases. It occurs abundantly in the liver of fish (Cod), in green leaves, green vegetables, or jam, butter and milk. It is deficient in most patent foods. Vitamin A is slowly destroyed by cooking.

Vitamin A is high in butter, cabbage, carrots, cheese, green beans, lemon juice, lettuce, raw peaches, fresh peas, pineapple, pumpkin, raw cabbage, sweet potatoes, raw tomatoes, wheaten bread, wheat bran, wheat grain. It is abundant in Cod-liver oil, cream, eggs, condensed milk, fresh milk, fresh spinach.

Vitamin B (anti-neuritic Vitamin): Water soluble. Nuts, seeds, lettuce, celery, etc., eggs, milk, vegetables, contain this Vitamin. Absence of vitamin B causes Beri-beri. This vitamin consists of two distinct components B-1 and B-2. B-1 is also known as Vitamin F and B-2 as vitamin G or P or P-1 (Pellagra preventive). The absence of B-2 leads to pellagra.

Vitamin B is high in almonds, apple, butter, buttermilk, cabbage, cauliflower, cheese, cocoanuts, cream, green leaves, lemon juice, lettuce, maize, condensed milk, fresh milk, oats, onions, orange juice, parsnip, fresh peas, raw pineapple, potatoes, rye, turnip, walnut, whole bran, raw tomatoes, fresh spinach, raw cabbage, white beans, wheaten bread.

Vitamin C (anti-scorbutic vitamin): Water soluble. This is regarded as the anti-scorbutic vitamin. It occurs chiefly in orange, lemon, cabbage, tomato. It is present in fresh vegetables, green leaves and fruits. Vitamin C deficiency leads to changes in the teeth and to scurvy. This vitamin is destroyed by cooking, storing and tinning.

Vitamin C is high in apple, fresh milk, onions, raw peaches, pineapple, potatoes. It is abundant in lemon-juice, lettuce, orange-juice, fresh peas, pineapple, raspberries, cabbage, spinach, turnip, raw tomatoes.

Vitamin D (anti-rachitic vitamin): Fat soluble. This is present in Cod-liver oil, cream, green vegetables, yolk of egg and butter. It is found in abundance in Cod-liver oil. Deficiency of this vitamin leads to rickets in children, Osteomalacia in pregnant women, defective dentition and caries of teeth. It helps in the maintenance of normal structure of bones and teeth. This vitamin controls phosphorus-calcium balance.

Vitamin D is high in fresh milk. It is abundant in Cod-liver oil. It is present in bread, cocoanuts, lettuce, condensed milk, fresh peas.

Vitamin E (anti-sterile vitamin): This is fat soluble. This is present principally in wheat germ, lettuce leaves, seeds and green leaves. It occurs in a less degree in milk, meat and whole wheat. The vitamin is anti-sterile. The addition of the vitamin produces normal fertility in rats.

## STORY OF VITAMIN A

### 1. INTRODUCTION

Adorations to the Lord, the source of vitamin A.

Man cannot live by calories alone. Diets of protein, carbohydrate, fat, minerals and water cannot support growth without the addition of some minute amount of a natural food such as milk. Natural foods contain a new kind of essential factor (Vitamin) which had previously been unsuspected.

It was Dr. Funk who gave us the marvellously convenient word "Vitamin". He used it first in 1912. One of the pioneers in this field was Lunin of Switzerland (1881). Other workers were Osborne and Mendel in the United States (1911) and Steep in Germany (1911). In 1912, Sir Fredhic Gowland Hopkins concluded by experiments on rats that milk contained "accessory food factors" which are essential for normal growth.

The amount of Vitamin necessary for health is exceedingly small compared with the total daily ration of food, and yet this small trace of vitamins makes all the difference to growth and the proper working of our bodies. Further deficiencies in the supply of Vitamins lead to actual disease. This idea is now perfectly familiar; but twenty-five years ago it was considered as a revolutionary theory or doctrine.

Each Vitamin has its own definite function. One Vitamin helps the formation of bones and teeth. Another vitamin strengthens the nervous system, while a third is indispensable to the growth and development of the body. The absence or deficiency of vitamins affects health, growth and reproduction. But if you take plenty of milk, butter, fruits and leafy vegetables, there will be no vitamin deficiency. You will have wonderful health, vim, vigour and vitality.

The Vitamin A from marine plants is obtained in a rather round-about way. Little-Shell-fishes feed on the marine plants. They themselves are then eaten by small fish. These in turn are eaten by big fish like the Cod or the Shark. When anyone eats the Cod fish or drinks the Cod or Shark liver oil, he eats his quota of Vitamin A.

Animals get Vitamin A by eating plants which contain Vitamin A. Vitamin A enters into the fat of their bodies where it is dissolved and stored. It is also stored in the liver. It is passed into the milk of animals who suckle their young.

Nursing mothers should take plenty of green vegetables and other foods, which contain Vitamin A. If they do not take these stuffs, the children are very weak at birth and during infancy. They are likely to contract diseases readily. Nursing mothers do not take the right kind of food which contains abundant Vitamin A. That is the reason why many children in India die in infancy.

## II. SOURCE

Vitamin A is found in animal fats, milk, curd, butter, ghee, egg yolk, liver, fish oils. Its richest known natural source is the liver oil of certain fish.

Cod-liver oil, Halibut-liver-oil, lose their Vitamin A if they are exposed to Sunlight. Therefore they should be kept in light-proof bottles.

Ordinary cooking does not destroy Vitamin A to any great

extent. It is only destroyed when the cooking is prolonged and if the food is exposed to the air during cooking.

Shark and Saw fish liver oil are richer in Vitamin A than Cod-liver oil, though not as rich as Halibut-liver oil.

Prolonged heating of ghee in open jars causes serious destruction of Vitamin A. Vegetable ghee and groundnut oil do not contain Vitamin A. The Vitamin A value of pure Cow's ghee is between 1000 and 2500 international units per gramme. The Vitamin A contained in different samples of butter varies from 800 to 6000 international units per 100 grammes.

Whole rice contains a little Vitamin A; when rice is milled and polished, even this little Vitamin is removed. When the parboiled heated rice is exposed to the air, the vitamin A is destroyed.

Vitamin A is produced when grains are sprouted after soaking in water. Sprouted dhals and gram contain Vitamin A in great abundance.

Polished rice, parboiled rice, vegetable oils, margarine, cocogem, vegetable ghees, mustard and almond oils do not contain any vitamin A.

Soya bean, dhals, gram, pea, beans, wheat, oats, barley, whole rice, potato, bananas, nuts, cocoanut oil, orange juice, groundnut oil, lard, contain a small quantity of Vitamin A. Red Palm oil is rich in Vitamin A but not in Vitamin D.

### III. FUNCTION

Vitamin A is made by the action of Sunlight on the green leaves of plants. It is required for the growth and repair of the body. Therefore it is necessary for children. It preserves the body from infectious diseases by keeping the mucous membrane and skin in a healthy condition. It keeps the blood in proper composition. It prevents water collecting in the tissues.

Vitamin A is the anti-xerotic Vitamin or anti-infective. It prevents xerophthalmia and various other similar troubles. Xerosis is a kind of dried up condition of the membranes of the body, which occurs when Vitamin A is absent. When the mucous membrane dries up, it breaks down, and microbes gain entry into the system through broken mucous membranes, and infectious diseases are produced.

Vitamin A works primarily on the eyes, the skin, and the membranes which line internal organs like the lungs and the digestive system. In 1916 and 1917, in Denmark, Margarine was used instead of butter, and 78 and 81 cases of eye disease were reported in these two years. In 1918 and 1919 butter was used instead of margarine. The number of cases of eye disease reported was reduced to 7 and 4, respectively. A diet low in Vitamin A causes colitis or inflammation of the colon, which forms a portion of the large intestines.

Children suffer from night blindness on account of lack of Vitamin A. Even a normally healthy man who can see all right during the day loses his eyesight when it is dark. This is night blindness. Night blindness can be cured quickly if a lot of Vitamin A is taken.

One is able to see properly on account of the presence of a peculiar colouring matter called the Visual purple found in the retina of the eye. If Vitamin A is deficient, this purple matter vanishes. Give Vitamin A. The visual purple appears again. You can see normally within a few hours. Vitamin A is required for the rejuvenation of the visual purple.

Normal structure of the teeth is not possible without an abundant supply of Vitamin A. The gums undergo structural changes on account of lack of sufficient Vitamin A. Pyorrhoea is due to lack of Vitamin A.

Vitamin A is needed for the growth and repair of the body in children and adults. Its chief function is concerned with nutrition of cells. Thus is raised the bodily resistance to diseases.

### IV. DEFICIENCY DISEASES

Deficiency of Vitamin A produces dry or rough skin, often called "toad skin", because it looks like the skin of a frog or toad. This skin disease occurs in Ceylon.

Vitamin A is absent in white bread and deficient in most patent and proprietary foods.

Vitamin A is fat soluble. Lack of Vitamin A causes

retardation of growth and susceptibility to bacterial infection of the eyes. Vitamin A is more necessary to mothers when nursing infants than at any other time.

A well-balanced diet should contain a daily minimum of 3000 international units. Three ounces of spinach leaves will supply 3000 international units.

Lack of Vitamin A produces stunted growth, eye and respiratory diseases (such as Pneumonia, Broncho-Pneumonia), constipation, cold, diarrhoea, dysentery, dropsy, stone in the bladder. An eye disease called keratomalacia (Xerophthalmia), which is a common cause of blindness in some parts of India, Ceylon, Malaysia, Java, Sumatra and China, is produced by persistent lack of Vitamin A. Many children are rendered blind on account of this disease.

## V. CAROTENE

Vegetable foods do not contain Vitamin A, but the pigment "Carotene" or "Pro-Vitamin A", which is present in many vegetable foods, is able to perform the functions of Vitamin A in the body.

Leafy vegetables such as spinach, lettuce, watercress, asparagus, broccoli, cabbage, amaranth leaves, coriander leaves, drumstick leaves, bamboo tops, radish tops, turnip tops, beet-root tops, celery leaves, and ripe fruits such as mangoes, papaya, tomatoes, oranges, etc., and sweet potatoes, carrots, are rich in carotene.

Carotene is found in yellow and orange coloured vegetables, fruits, apricots and peaches (fresh and dried), sweet potatoes, pumpkin, squash and yellow maize.

Cooking has no effect on carotene.

An enzyme or ferment in the liver changes carotene into Vitamin A. It is stored in the body and is comparatively stable.

In milk and milk products, the amount of both Vitamin A and carotene depends on whether the cow has a good supply of carotene in its food or not. When the cows eat green grass and leaves, there is plenty of Vitamin A and carotene in milk. When the cows eat dry grass and roots, there is not much of these factors in the milk. Such milk is not suitable for children. Milk can be made rich in Vitamin A, if the cows are fed on carrot or food which contains abundance of carotene.

When you eat carotene it is changed into Vitamin A in the body. Hence carotene is known as pro-Vitamin A. Carotene and Vitamin A are intimately related. The yellower follower to plants were, the more Vitamin A actually they had. Yellow pigment, carotene, which is found in yellow and orange coloured plant food, has properties identical with those of Vitamin A.

A good indication of the carotene content of leafy vegetables is their greenness. The greener the better, and the fresher the better. All green leafy vegetables are rich in carotene. Other vegetables, cereals, legumes, etc., are less important sources of carotene.

## VI. CONCLUSION

Vitamin A deficiency is common in India. Great care must be taken to ensure that diets provide an adequate supply of this Vitamin.

He who dwells in this Vitamin A, who is within this Vitamin A, whom the Vitamin A does not know, whose body the Vitamin is, who rules the Vitamin A from within is thy own Inner Self, Atman, Inner Ruler, Immortal, (Antaryamin, Amrita). Glory to the Creator of Vitamin A. May His blessings be upon you all!

## TALE OF VITAMIN B

### I. INTRODUCTION

Adorations to the Lord, the source of vitamin B.

Vitamin B was originally supposed to be one composite element. But it has been found that there is quite a variety of B Vitamins, which are now named B-1 and the B-2 group, respectively.

Vitamin B-1 is a water-soluble vitamin. It is commonly known as the "anti-Beri-beri vitamin" and also as "Theamine" and "Aneurin". It is also known as "Anti-neuritic vitamin". It is not stored in the body. It contains sulphur in its molecule. As vitamin B-1 is soluble in water, food that contains this vitamin should not be soaked in water. It should be cooked conservatively and the water used for soups, etc. Much washing of rice dissolves the vitamin B-1. It is lost in this way.

Cooking foods which contain Vitamin B-1 with alkaline substances, e.g., soda, destroys it. Cooking lessens it appreciably, but does not destroy it.

A diet largely composed of raw, milled rice contains insufficient vitamin B-1 and causes Beri-beri. Parboiled rice, even when highly milled, usually contains Vitamin B enough to prevent Beri-beri. Even if milled rice is eaten, there is not much danger of Beri-beri, if 3 ozs of pulses are taken daily.

Experiments were made on pigeons. Polished rice is lacking in Vitamin B-1, which is present in unpolished rice. Those fed on polished rice began to lose their appetite, became very thin, suffered from diarrhoea, got paralysis and died. But if to the polished rice were added the rice polishings in time, then the tragedy was averted.

A dog suffering from marked paralysis of the hind legs as the result of a diet lacking in Vitamin B-1 was cured in a short time by supply of vitamin B in the form of tomato juice.

Just as insufficiency of Vitamin A in food is responsible for rickets, insufficiency of Vitamin B is responsible for Beri-beri. Beri-beri is a disease that is found amongst people whose staple food is rice. The disease has been greatly on an increase owing to the introduction of machine-milling, which destroys the nutritive value of all grains and cereals. Bradycardia, or slow heat rate, is caused by excess of Lactic acid. Lactic acid poisons the muscles of the heart and prevents its functioning at full rate. Excess of Lactic acid cannot be removed without Vitamin B-1. If you give Vitamin B-1, the Lactic acid is eliminated from the system, and the heart begins to function normally. It regains its normal rate again.

Adults who live on ordinary diets in ordinary circumstances require 350 international units per day. If you take more carbohydrates, you need more Vitamin B-1. Fats exercise a Vitamin B-1 action sparingly. If you take whole wheat, any of the millets or whole cereal grain, home pounded rice and parboiled rice, milk, dhal, tomatoes, green leafy vegetables, tuber and root vegetables, you will have an abundant supply of Vitamin B-1.

There must be abundant Vitamin B-1, in the food of nursing mothers. Otherwise the children may get diseases.

Plants extract from the soil and air some substances and produce the Vitamin B-1 from those substances. It is present chiefly in the seed or fruit of the plants and green leaves. When these parts are eaten by man and animals, the Vitamin B-1 is absorbed into their system and utilised for their growth and repair of their tissues and the various processes of digestion, elimination and muscular and nervous action.

## II. SOURCE

Yeast, marmite and the outer layers of cereals removed on milling, e.g., rice and wheat bran, contain abundant Vitamin B-1. The richest sources of Vitamin B-1 are pulses, peas, beans, lentils, dhals, gram, nuts, such as walnuts, and unmilled cereals (wheat, barley, maize, cholam, cambu and ragi), green leafy vegetables such as spinach, turnip tops, radish tops, lettuce, watercress, celery, asparagus and tomatoes, and eggs.

Wheat, barley, maize, cholam, kambu, ragi, oats, oatmeal, beans, peas, dhals, gram, soya bean, nuts of all kinds, cabbage, carrots, turnips, beetroot tops, contain much Vitamin B-1.

The largest quantum of Vitamin B is present in the germ (embryo) of wheat and other cereals. There is a certain amount in the bran, but the endosperm which occupies most of the gram is deficient in Vitamin B-1. Wholemeal brown flour contains Vitamin B-1, but white flour contains little or none, as the bran and embryo are removed during the process of milling, just as they are with polished rice. From the point of view of Vitamin B-1 content, wholemeal bread is thought superior to white bread.

There is a small amount of Vitamin B-1 in many foods. Vitamin B-1 can also be made synthetically in the laboratory. These synthetic preparations are used for the treatment of patients who suffer from neuritis and lack of appetite.

Animal tissues are much lesser rich than plants in Vitamin B-1. Plants are able to synthesise it.

Meat, fish, eggs, vegetables, white bread; whole rice, parboiled rice, bananas, beet root, brinjal, potato, radish, sweet potatoes, fruits, grapes, dates, lemons, oranges, papaya, pears, prunes and milk are poor in Vitamin B-1. Vitamin B-1 is not found in white sugar. A little is present in brown sugar or jaggery and in honey.

White flour, polished rice, butter, cheese, sugar, starch, tea, coffee, honey, all animal and vegetable fats and oils contain no or very little vitamin B-1.

## III. FUNCTION

Vitamin B is growth-promoting and prevents Beri-beri and neuritis. It stimulates appetite. It is essential for maintaining the normal tone of the digestive tract both in the stomach and intestines. It regulates the use of carbohydrate in the body. It indirectly affects growth by increasing the quantity of food taken. It is very essential for health and the well-being of man. It keeps the body well. Vitamin B is necessary throughout life.

It controls the activity of the intestinal tract, stimulates the digestive glands, increases the utilisation of foodstuff and prevents bacterial infections. It is required for the building and the repair of the body. It keeps the brain, nerves, the heart, the liver, the digestive glands, the kidneys, the muscles of the body including those of the bowels, healthy and strong. It maintains the appetite and the digestion. Waste materials are discharged properly from the body. It maintains the proper action of the muscles, nerves, and skin. If the food contains abundant Vitamin B, it is exceedingly palatable.

## IV. DEFICIENCY DISEASES

Deficiency or absence of Vitamin B-1 causes Beri-beri, indigestion, diarrhoea, constipation and pain in the belly. The muscles become weak and the nerves are irritable. Resistance to infectious diseases is decreased.

Much of the malnutrition of children is due to lack of sufficient Vitamin B-1 in their diets. If extra Vitamin B is given, baby gains weight. Milk is not a very rich source of Vitamin B.

A deficiency of Vitamin B-1 stunts the body. Failure to gain weight normally is due to Vitamin B-1 deficiency.

## V. BERI-BERI

The legs become weak and helpless. The heart may fail in its task of pumping blood all round the body, there is partial or complete paralysis of the limbs due to degeneration of the nerves. There is swelling or dropsy of the limbs and trunk, and weakness of heart muscle leading to failure of the heart.

Until a comparatively recent date it was held that Beri-beri was of microbic or toxic origin and ought, therefore, to be placed among the infectious diseases. It is now recognised that the disease is of nutritional origin due to the absence of the water-soluble vitamin B-1 from the food. It occurs mainly among rice-consuming people, and therefore the relationship of rice to its production was first investigated. When white or polished rice forms the main ingredient of the dietary, Beri-beri frequently develops. It is rare when the whole grain is used. Cases which have occurred on a polished rice dietary can be cured by the use of the whole grain.

The pericarp, aleurone layer and germ of the rice contain the Vitamin B-1. These are all removed by milling. The administration of an extract of the millings is sufficient to cure the disease.

But Beri-beri also occurs in certain instances where the dietary does not consist of polished rice, on board ship for example, and among the labourers of a Brazilian railway, whose diet consisted mainly of tinned vegetables and white flour. The Vitamin is readily destroyed by heating to above 100 degrees centigrade. The high degree of heat needed in the sterilisation of tinned food is quite sufficient to destroy it totally.

The chief habitation of the disease is Japan, China, Malaya, Archipelago, Burma, Brazil, the Philippine Islands, the Andhra area in Southern India. Males between 15 and 25 are oftenest attacked but neither sex nor age is exempted.

There are two types of this disease. The dry or paralytic and dropsical or wet. There is less of knee jerks in the dry variety. In the beginning it is increased. The patient becomes thin and emaciated. At first there is difficulty in walking, with the characteristic high stepping gait of foot drop. In the wet form, a pit or hollow is temporarily produced if the swollen part is pressed with the fingers. There are palpitation, difficulty of breathing. The heart is enlarged on the right side.

Make the patient squat down. Those in whom the disease is beginning will be unable to rise.

Alteration of the faulty diet is the essential measure in the treatment of Beri-beri. Yeast or marmite, extract of the millings, should be given. The use of undermilled, instead of polished rice is the chief prophylactic measure. It has done away with Beri-beri in the Siam Government institutions.

He who dwells in this Vitamin B, who is within this Vitamin B whom the Vitamin B does not know, whose body the Vitamin is, who rules the vitamin B from within, is thy own Inner Self, Atman, Inner Ruler, Immortal, Antaryami, Amritam.

Glory to the Creator of Vitamin B. May His blessings be upon you all.

## VITAMIN B-2 OR G

### I. INTRODUCTION

Adorations to the Lord, the source of vitamin B-2.

The Vitamin B-2 group or complex is of great importance in human nutrition. The group includes nicotinic acid, flavin, vitamin B-6 and other constituents. Vitamin B-2 is known as Vitamin G or P-P-1 (Pellagra preventive).

This is water-soluble. It is less soluble in water but more heat-resisting than B-1. Vitamin G is usually accompanied by Vitamin B-1. It is stored to a small extent in the liver. As it is soluble in water, it is considerably lessened by cooking with water. Soda in the water makes the loss of the Vitamin still greater.

The Flavin factor, which is often called Vitamin B-2 in England and Vitamin G in the United States, is one of the Vitamins from the Vitamin B complex. Flavin is a greenish yellow substance. Lacto-flavin has been obtained from milk, ovo-flavin from egg-white and hepato-flavin from liver.

Other Vitamins that have come from the B complex are Vitamins B-3, B-4, B-5 and B-6 (or H). They have appeared during work on laboratory animals. There is no evidence yet that they are necessary for human beings.

## II. SOURCE

Yeast, milk products (buttermilk, curds, cheese, skimmed milk), whole cereals, pulses, green leafy vegetables are the best sources for Vitamin B-2.

Milled cereals, and in particular raw milled rice, vegetables and fruits in general, are very poor in Vitamin B-2.

## III. FUNCTION

Vitamin B-2 is essential to growth and general well-being. Its presense favours early maturity and delays the onset of old age. It helps to keep the eyes, tongue and intestines in a healthy condition. Lack or absence of Vitamin B-2 produces Pellagra, a kind of skin disease. Vitamin B-2 plays a vital part in blood formation and so is intimately concerned in oxidation.

## IV. DEFICIENCY DISEASES

Maize is almost totally deficient in Vitamin B-2. Therefore a disease known as Pellagra breaks out among those maize-eating people who are unable to make up the deficiency by taking a mixed diet. Pellagra occurs most commonly in those whose diet consists largely of milled rice.

Soreness of the angles of the mouth and of the tongue is caused by deficiency of Vitamins belonging to the B-2 complex. If 1 oz. of dried yeast or 1 pound of milk is given, the soreness disappears.

Vitamin B-2 deficiency results in digestion disturbances, inadequate blood formation, a lack of resistance to infectious diseases and general lack of vitality.

## V. PELLAGRA

It is prevalent also among the poor people in the south-eastern countries of Europe and in the cotton belt of the United States of America. In one year, 1746 people of U.S.A. died of the disease. The disease is met with in countries surrounding the Mediterranean Sea and in the Southern States of

America. Of late years cases have also been recognised in Britain.

It is a disease characterised by a chronic erythematous eruption, digestive disturbances and nervous symptoms, and associated with the consumption of maize.

Pellagra is practically unknown in Northern Europe but it is a formidable scourge in countries where maize is the staple foodstuff. There is a certain amount of Pellagra in Italy, Rumania and Africa, and a great deal in the southern part of the United States. The word "Pellagra" means rough skin. The victims of the disease are called "Pellagrins". They suffer from a peculiar type of inflammation of the skin.

Zein, the chief protein of maize does not contain two essential amino-acids (tryptophane and lysine). It was at one time thought that Pellagra might be due to amino-acid deficiency. But Dr. Goldberger, who was working in the United States, found that yeast and several other foods contained a factor which resembles a vitamin and which is capable of curing Pellagra. He called this the P-P (Pellagra-preventive) factor. He found that it was present in liver, wheat-germ, egg-yolk, meat and yeast. The P-P factor was once thought to be identical with Vitamin B-2 or G, but later work showed that this was not so.

Pellagra can be cured by administering nicotinic acid, a derivative of the nicotinic tobacco.

Pellagra was regarded as due to deficiency of air amino-acid (tryptophane) in the dietary, but is now recognised as due to the absence of B-2 Vitamin.

Digestive disturbances and disability are followed by an erythematous eruption. It recurs every spring. There is very troublesome itching. It lasts about a fortnight and leaves the skin, roughened, scaly and pigmented. There is great emaciation. Give a varied, generous and well-balanced diet, the disease is cured.

## VI. VITAMIN B-2 THERAPY

Give a balanced diet. Give sufficient quantity of milk, curds. cheese, buttermilk, leafy vegetables such as spinach, whole cereal and pulses. All the diseases which result from Vitamin B-2 deficiency will be cured.

He who dwells in this Vitamin B-2, who is within this Vitamin B-2, whom the Vitamin B-2 does not know, whose body the Vitamin is, who rules the Vitamin B-2 from within, is thy own Inner Self, Atman, Inner Ruler, Immortal, Antaryami, Amritam.

Glory to the Creator of Vitamin B-2. May His blessings be upon you all.

## VITAMIN C (ANALYSED)
### 1. INTRODUCTION

Adorations to the Lord, the source of Vitamin C.

Vitamin C or ascorbic acid is water soluble. It is known as anti-scorbutic vitamin as it acts against scurvy and cures it. It was noticed that sailors used to suffer from a disease called scurvy during long voyages when they could not get fresh vegetables and fruits to eat. In this disease the gums become sore and bleed, the legs swell and pain. This is prevented or those suffering from this illness recover, if they are given the juice of lemons. This is because green leaves, vegetables and fruits contain another Vitamin called C. This vitamin is destroyed by cooking, storing and tinning, drying by heat above 60 degrees centigrade and by alkalies. It is protected by acids.

Navigators constantly noted the curative effect of oranges and lemons and in 1804 a regular issue of lemon juice was made compulsory in the British Navy, after which Scurvy became rare.

In the Great War, Von Luckner escaped with a group of men in a small boat and spent weeks sailing in the Pacific Ocean. When the men finally landed at a small island, all were suffering from advanced scurvy. They had a diet of fresh food, mainly fruits for a few days. They were completely cured.

The final proof that Scurvy is a deficiency disease, caused by the lack of some factor present in fresh fruit vegetables, was provided by Holstein and Frolick in 1907-1912. Some years later, the Anti-Scurvy or Anti-Scorbutic factor was given the name of Vitamin C.

# VITAMIN C (ANALYSED)

In order to obtain the maximum amount of Vitamin C, both fruits and vegetables should be as fresh as possible. Freshly dug potatoes contain about three times as much Vitamin C as those which have been stored in shops. The peel of oranges and lemons contains even more Vitamin C than the juice.

A certain amount of Vitamin C is lost during cooking, but if cooking is short, the loss will not be serious.

Vitamin C is preserved in oranges, lemons and tomatoes on account of their acid contents.

As Vitamin C is destroyed in cooking, raw fruits and vegetables should be included in the diet daily.

Soda should not be added in cooking as it destroys the Vitamin. Of all the Vitamins, C is most easily destroyed by heat. All children should get orange juice or tomato juice.

## II. SOURCE

Oranges, lemons, grapes, most fresh fruits, straw-berries, pineapples, tomatoes, cabbages, all fresh green vegetables and sprouted pulses are good sources of Vitamin C. Raw cabbage is as good as orange.

A particularly rich source of the Vitamin is Amla or Nellikai (Phyllanthus emblica). One Amla fruit contains as much vitamin as one or two oranges. The heating or drying of fresh fruits or vegetables causes destruction of most or all of the Vitamin C. But the Vitamin of Amla is not destroyed by heating or drying as it contains substances which protect the Vitamin and as its juice is very strong acid. Acidity has a protective action on Vitamin C. Therefore Amla can be nicely preserved. It can be cut into pieces, dried in the Sun quickly and then powdered. But most Vitamin is lost when the Amla is boiled and fried in oil and salt and curry powder are added.

Amla is a tonic. It enters into the composition of Chyavanaprash and Triphala Choorna. It is an ingredient in many Ayurvedic medicines and tonics.

Fresh Amla is a good preventive against Scurvy. It is an effective cure for Scurvy when there is shortage of fruit and vegetables. Amla can be taken with much advantage.

When fresh vegetables and fruits are not easily obtained, sprouted greens may be used. This is a cheap and easily available source of Vitamin C. Sprouted pulses contain 10-15 milligrammes of Vitamin C per 100 grammes. The sprouted greens should be eaten raw or after cooking for not more than 10 minutes.

Pulses and cereal grains do not contain any Vitamin C in the ordinary state. When they are allowed to sprout, the Vitamin is formed in the grain and in the growing green sprouts.

The peel of oranges and lemons, apples and pears, asparagus, fresh carrots, lettuce, water cress, turnip tops, celery, raw potato, sprouted beans, sprouted peas, contain a good deal of Vitamin C.

Milk, skimmed milk, buttermilk, curds, cooked potato, banana, apples, pears are poor in Vitamin C.

Soya beans, oatmeal, wheat flour, barley, dried peas, beans, dhal, gram, cholam, ragi, cambu, maize, sugar, honey, vegetable oils, dried fruits of all kinds, dried vegetables of all kinds, nuts of all kinds, tinned fruit, tinned milk contain no or very little Vitamin C.

The Vitamin C that is supplied by 4 pints of milk, 2 lbs of turnips or grapes, 1 lb of carrots, ½ lb of apples or bananas or potatoes, is supplied by one ounce of lemon or orange juice or fresh cabbage leaves.

### III. FUNCTION

Vitamin C is necessary for keeping good health in general. It acts on the skin. It is a valuable substance in the forming of the blood. Vitamin C prevents infantile and adult scurvy.

It is necessary for proper tooth formation and for the prevention of pyorrhoea and tooth decay.

Vitamin C plays a vital part in the process of respiration and oxidation.

In infectious diseases Vitamin C is used in combating and neutralising the toxins and in the formation of specific anti-bodies. Vitamin C is required to keep the blood pure and of proper composition, to aid the other Vitamins in the building of the body, particularly the bones and the teeth, to keep the bowels

# VITAMIN C (ANALYSED)

healthy, to keep the teeth in good condition and to assist the body to resist infection by germs.

## IV. DEFICIENCY DISEASES

The lack of Vitamin C causes Scurvy, pains in the limbs, gangrene of gums and loss of teeth. Extreme lack causes disease, while less marked lack produces lassitude, weakness and poor appetite.

Retardation of growth in children, irritability and general lack of vigour is due to a lack of Vitamin C. Fresh fruits and vegetables should be added to the diet of children.

When Scurvy is present, susceptibility to bacterial infection is increased.

## V. SCURVY

This is a nutritional disorder characterised by great debility, a spongy condition of the gums, a tendency to haemorrage and anaemia or bloodlessness. It is usually associated with improper and insufficient food. The old theories of the causation are that it is due to an undiscovered specific micro-organism, that it is due to a deficiency of the inorganic or organic salts found in fresh fruits and vegetables, that it is due to poisoning by a ptomaine produced by the decomposition of food. They have been abandoned since the discovery of an accessory food factor, differing from fat-soluble A and water-soluble B and known as the anti-scorbutine Vitamin C.

Symptoms are at first insidious. The patient becomes weak, breathless, drowsy or languid, with general aching of the bones and joints. The gums are soft and swollen, bleeding easily on the slightest pressure. As the disease progresses, the teeth may fall out. The heart is irregular. The patient is rendered quite unfit for mental or physical exertion.

## VI. INFANTILE SCURVY

This is known by the name Barlow's disease. This sometimes occurs in children brought up on proprietary foods. It is most frequent between the sixth and the twentieth month. There are anaemia, debility. The gums are swollen and spongy. The lower limbs are tender. The child is unwilling to move.

Cow's milk and fresh fruit juices (orange juice, lemon juice) will cure the disease.

## VII. VITAMIN C THERAPY

Scurvy can be cured by supplying vitamin C. Diet should consist of fresh milk, cream, etc., the juice of two or three fresh lemons or oranges. Preserved lime-juice is useless. Fresh fruits and vegetables should be liberally given; but vegetables must not be cooked with soda.

A well-balanced diet should contain 25 to 45 mgs. of vitamin C per day. Fruit juice (lemon juice or orange juice) should be given to children.

If you drink orange juice, caries of teeth will be checked. Gingivitis or inflammation of the gums due to pyorrhoea will be cured. A man requires daily the amount of Vitamin C in 60 CC of orange juice.

He who dwells in this Vitamin C, who is within this Vitamin C, whom the Vitamin C does not know, whose body the Vitamin C is, who rules the Vitamin C from within, is thy own Inner Self, Atman, Inner Ruler, Immortal, Antaryami, Amritam.

Glory to the Creator of Vitamin C. May His blessings be upon you all.

## VITAMIN D (ANALYSED)

### I. INTRODUCTION

Adorations to the Lord, the source of Vitamin D.

Vitamin D is fat-soluble. It is the Vitamin which prevents rickets and osteomalaria. Rickets is a disease of darkness. It is associated with food which is wanting in Vitamin D, which is usually present in milk, butter, eggs or cod-liver oil. A child living in a dark house, who does not get enough milk or who is fed on milk from a cow that has been kept in a dark stable contracts this disease. But if the child lives in open Sunlight or the milk and cow are exposed to sufficient Sunlight, then the disease does not occur.

The story of the discovery of Vitamin D is most interesting. It has brought out most clearly the co-relation between darkness and disease.

Vitamin D is found in association with Vitamin A and was at first thought to be identical with it. Later on, it was found that certain foods and the skin upon exposure to Sunlight develop the same property. It is stable to heat and can be stored in the body.

## II. SOURCE

Anti-rachitic Vitamin D is found in whole milk, milk products like butter, ghee, eggs and some fish oils. Cod-liver oil, Halibut-liver oil are excellent sources. A little is preserved in cocoanut oil and peanut oil. It is not preserved in any other vegetable oil. There is another cheap and potent source of Vitamin D. That is the Sun. The action of the rays of the Sun on the skin manufactures this Vitamin. The Sunlight transforms a substance normally present in the skin, the precursor of Vitamin D, into Vitamin D itself. This explains how rickets and similar bone deformities may be cured by carefully directed exposure of the skin to Sunlight. Stand in the Sun and rub the body with gingily oil or mustard oil. Vitamin D gets into the body in this way. Expose the vegetable oils to the Sun before they are used as food.

There is no Vitamin D in plant foods. There is a minute amount in spinach.

## III. FUNCTION

Vitamin D controls phosphorus-calcium balance. It aids in the retention of calcium and phosphorus and controls the minerals in the blood. The body cannot fully utilise calcium and phosphorus, which are necessary for bone-formation, without the aid of Vitamin D. Vitamin D aids in absorbing calcium and phosphorus as well as their retention after absorption. It works primarily on the teeth and bones. An abundant intake of Vitamin D aids in the formation of strong regular teeth. A good supply of this Vitamin during pregnancy is beneficial to the mother. It is a great aid for the future development of the child.

## IV. DEFICIENCY DISEASES

Lack of Vitamin D is associated with bone deficiencies, e.g, rickets in early childhood and abnormal tooth development in older children. Want of sufficient Vitamin D in the food is one of the causes of bad teeth and of their early decay.

Osteomalacia or softening of the bones is a disease common among pregnant women. This is due to lack of calcium and Vitamin D. In these two diseases the bones become soft and bent. The patient becomes a cripple.

The researches of Lady Mellanby have shown that lack of Vitamin D is frequently associated with bad teeth. She found that decay of teeth could be checked even in badly formed teeth by a diet containing adequate amount of calcium, phosphorus, and Vitamin D. Cereals and cereal products were found, on the contrary, to hinder calcification.

## V. RICKETS

Only within the last twenty or thirty years have the doctors come to know that rickets is due to Vitamin D deficiency.

In 1918 Sir Edward Mellanby worked on puppies and found that both butter and Cod-liver oil contained an anti-rachitic factor which protected the puppies from rickets or cured the disease if given in time.

Rickets or Rachites is a disease of deficiency, due to absence of Vitamin D from the diet. It occurs in late infancy. There are wasting, stunted growth and deformities. Over-crowding, lack of fresh air, lack of Sunlight are contributory factors.

The fact that housing conditions appeared to affect the incidence of rickets is now attributed to the lack of Sunshine in slums. The idea that rickets was due to lack of fat is explained by saying that a diet deficient in fat would almost certainly be deficient in the fat-soluble, anti-rachitic Vitamin D. The suggestion that excess of cereals was responsible is now thought to be due either to the presence of a "toxamin" in the cereal (an anti-calcifying substance) or to the amount of phytin present (which prevents the use of calcium).

Rickets may arise if the food does not contain enough calcium and phosphorus or if these mineral elements are not present in the food in the right proportion, one to another. Rickets

# VITAMIN D (ANALYSED)

may also occur, if the food does not contain enough Vitamin D or if the body does not get enough Sunlight.

There must be enough building materials, viz., calcium and phosphorus, to make the bones. If the food does not contain enough calcium or phosphorus or if it contains too much phosphorus and too little calcium, then there are not enough building materials to make bones. In the construction of a building there must be enough building materials, lime, bajri or sand, brick, cement, surkhi, stone, etc. There must be good masons to construct the building. Then only will the building be Pukka or strong and beautiful. Such is the case with the construction of this body-building. If the masons are not able and efficient, the building will be spoiled even if you have enough building materials.

Even when there are enough building materials such as calcium and phosphorus, the builders, Vitamin D and Sunlight, may be absent or scanty, and so the building materials cannot be properly used. Rickets may develop in this way also.

You can obtain all the Vitamins from a few leafy vegetables. Milk, fresh fruit and fresh leafy vegetables are very important parts of your food, because they contain all the things, proteins, minerals, salts and Vitamins. If you take any cereal grain with milk, fresh fruit and fresh green leafy vegetables, you will have enough of suitable proteins, fats, carbohydrates, minerals, salts and vitamins. You will have wonderful health and amazing power to work. There will be no deficiency diseases of any kind.

## VI. OSTEOMALACIA

Mollitis ossium (osteomalacia) is a disorder of the bony system due to gradual decalcification and weakening of the skeleton, resulting ultimately in considerable deformities and contortions. It is a disease of the poor and is common in women in India between 25 and 35 years of age, mostly after pregnancy. Osteomalacia usually starts during pregnancy, when demands for calcium are increased on account of the needs of the growing child in the womb. There is bending of the bones. Spontaneous fractures and distortions may occur. The pelvic deformities cause difficult labour. The stature is diminished. She is not able to stand upright. Irradiated ergosterol, 2 to 5 mgms, three times daily, and Sunlight are curative.

## VII. VITAMIN D THERAPY

The child should be kept in fresh air and Sunshine. The essential point in the treatment of rickets is a sufficient supply of Vitamin D Cream and Cod-liver oil should be given. Ultra-violet light is beneficial. Irradiated ergosterol is given in tabloid form. Cod-liver oil is rubbed on the belly.

Rickets is preventable and curable by a diet sufficiently rich in Vitamin D, and by exposure to Sunlight or irradiation, thus forming Vitamin D from ergosterol in the skin. More Vitamin D is needed when the diet is rich in cereals. There is a toxic substance in the cereals (toxamin) which inhibits the action of Vitamin D. If the calcium-phosphorus proportion in the diet be kept at optimum level, rickets does not develop even in the absence of Vitamin D. If there is a deficiency of these, or a disproportion, more Vitamin D is necessary.

Take foods which contain ergosterol. Ergosterol is very widely distributed in all kinds of natural foodstuff. Take a Sun-bath. Let the ergosterol be activated in the skin by the ultra-violet rays of the Sun. This is the natural method of obtaining Vitamin D. Understand the health-giving properties of Sunlight and the vital part played by the skin. The skin is a reservoir of light. Wear light clothing and have an open air life. This will be conducive to good health.

Exposure of the skin to the ultra-violet end of the spectrum results in the formation of Vitamin D.

A mull-Vitamin D diet protects against rickets even in the absence of Sunlight. Irradiation of ergosterol with ultra-violet light results in the production of a substance possessing marked anti-rachitic activity.

Ergosterol is, therefore, regarded as "Pro-Vitamin D". The synthetic preparation (pure Vitamin D) thus obtained is named "Calciferol" (because it helps to calcify Bones and teeth). Irradiated ergosterol seems to be slightly different from the naturally occurring Vitamin D of fish-liver oil. It is called Vitamin D-2. Calciferol is amazingly active. Less than half an ounce is enough to supply the daily ration of Vitamin D for a lifetime.

It is better to use natural products whenever possible. There is no risk of obtaining too much Vitamin D in natural products. Care should be taken to avoid an overdose in synthetic preparations, which contain concentrated Vitamin D. Enormous overdoses are toxic. They may have serious bad effects, such as hardening of the arteries, kidney stones and strong deposits in many parts of the body (Hypervitaminosis). Adhere strictly to the dose on the bottle.

Sun-bathing should not be overdone. In Sunless climates it is necessary to give Vitamin D to babies.

Various foods can be irradiated to make good sources of Vitamin D. A thin layer of food is exposed to ultra-violet light at a distance of above 2 feet. Lard, butter, milk, vegetable oils, cereals have all been treated in this way.

Extra Vitamin D is required by pregnant and nursing mothers and children, to ensure good development of teeth and to prevent rickets.

Feed the baby on a dried milk preparation in which the right amount of Vitamin D has already been added by the manufacturers. Excess of Vitamin D will bring excess of calcium and phosphorus to the blood (overcalcification).

## VII. SUNLIGHT

Sunlight plays a vital part in the cure of rickets. Rickets never occur in the tropics. Even in England it was less common in summer than in winter. The effect of ultra-violet light and Sunlight is the same as the addition of Vitamin D to the diet. This was experimented by Dr. Hess in the United States and Dr. Huldschinsky in Germany. Sunlight could not effect a complete cure in serious cases unless the diet contained a certain amount of Vitamin D. The action of the rays of the Sun on the skin manufactures the Vitamin D. That is one reason why people in Southern and Central India, where the Sunlight is very strong, do not suffer from rickets or osteomalacia, which people in North, particularly women who are kept behind the purdah are its worst victims. Sun-bathing should not be overdone. In Sunless climates it is necessary to give Vitamin D to babies.

He who dwells in this Vitamin D, who is within this Vitamin D, whom the Vitamin D does not know, whose body the Vitamin D is, who rules the Vitamin D from within, is thy own Inner Self, Atman, Inner Ruler, Immortal, Antaryami, Amritam.

Glory to the Creator of Vitamin D. May His blessings be upon you all.

## VITAMIN E (ANALYSED)

### I. INTRODUCTION

Adorations to the Lord, the source of Vitamin E.

Vitamin E is fat-soluble. Vitamin E is not easily destroyed by heat. Its discovery arose from experimental work on rats. On certain diets, acknowledged to be rich in Vitamin A, B, C, D, rats grew, but were sterile. The addition of Vitamin E produced normal fertility.

### II. SOURCE

This Vitamin is richly present in wheat-germ oil and, to a less degree, in milk, meat, lettuce, water-cress, whole-wheat, wheat, wheat-germs, whole-meal bread, olive oil and greens.

### III. FUNCTION

It is known as the anti-sterility vitamin. It is essential for reproduction. In its absence, degeneration of the seminiforous tubules of the male and the cessation of pregnancy, with abortion, in the female occur.

He who dwells in this Vitamin E, who is within this Vitamin E, whom the Vitamin E does not know, whose body the Vitamin E is, who rules the Vitamin E from within, is thy own Inner Self, Atman, Inner Ruler, Immortal, Antaryami, Amritam.

## THE STORY OF VITAMINS
### "A"

I am Vitamin A, enemy of germs.
I live in milk, butter and curd.
I keep the skin healthy.

I remove night-blindness.
If you miss me in your food,
I will give you bad eyesight.
I am needed for growth and repair of body.
I will make your skin beautiful.
I will give you good eyesight.
Nursing mothers need me more .
To keep their children healthy and strong.
Goodbye, friends! Be cheerful!
I shall meet you again at the dining table.

### "B"

I am Vitamin B, the foe of "Beri-beri",
I belong to a complex group.
B-2, B-3, B-4, B-5, B-6 (H) are my brothers,
Do not cook me with soda,
I will run away immediately,
I am abundant in Marmite and bran,
I had my abode in the paddy,
When people crushed me in the mill,
I left my original home at once.
I am growth-promoting.
I make the food extremely palatable.
I am essential for your health and well-being.
Do not miss me, comrade.
Take your Vitamin "B",
I shall keep you healthy and strong.

### "B-2 or G"

I am Vitamin B-2 or G, the enemy of Pellagra,
I am P-P-1 Pellagra-Preventive.
I am abundant in milk, cereals, pulses,
I am essential to growth and general well-being,
If you miss me in your food,
You will get Pellagra,
I will produce soreness of the mouth.
I am not present in raw milled rice and maize.
If you miss me at your dining table,
I will generate Pellagra.

Take a balanced diet, my child;
Take milk, spinach and curd,
There will be no B-2 deficiency,
You will be robust and healthy.

## "C"

I am the foe of Scurvy,
Which attacks the sailors,
And those who do not take vegetables.
I am abundant in orange juice,
Lemon juice and tomato juice.
If you miss me in your food,
I will make your gums bleed.
I enrich the blood.
If you cannot get lemon or orange,
Take Amla or Nellikai
I am very rich in this fruit,
Make Amla Murabba and take it daily.

## "D"

I am the enemy of rickets
And Osteomalacia.
I am present in milk and butter
I am "Ergosterol" and "Calciferol".
I build the bones.
I make use of Calcium and Phosphorus.
I supply you with Vitamin "D"
If you take in the Sun-bath,
I make your teeth strong and healthy.
If you expose your skin and food
To Ultra-violet light.
There I am in abundance.

## "E"

I am the foe of Sterility.
O sterile man, O barren woman,
Do not be afraid any more.
I shall remove your barrenness.
You will get healthy children.

Think of me and dance in joy.
You need not go to Ramesvaram,
And do Sarpa Santi.
You need not repeat Santana Mantra.
I am abundant in wheat germs,
Lettuce and whole-meal bread.
Take them freely.
I shall make you fertile.

## Chapter V
### DIETETIC PRINCIPLES

If you follow these dietetic rules you will surely attain wonderful health, longevity and high standard of vigour and vitality.

1. Fruits should be perfectly ripe. Do not eat sour or unripe fruits.

2. Eat only when you are really hungry. Beware of false hunger.

3. Eat less, masticate more. Masticate your food thoroughly. Chew every mouthful 30 times. Do not eat too rapidly. Do not bolt your food hastily.

4. Fast one day in a week. Fasting eliminates the poisons, overhauls the internal mechanism and gives rest to the organs.

5. Do not overload the stomach. Take Mitahara (moderate diet). Get up when three-quarter of the stomach is full.

6. Do not eat anything which you do not like, but do not eat everything which you like most.

7. Take always some raw vegetables like cucumber, radish, with your food. Reduce cooked food to a minimum.

8. Eat only 4 or 5 kinds of food at one meal. Abandon too many mixtures or combinations. It is difficult for the digestive juice to digest complex, diverse combinations.

9. Eat only combinations that are compatible. If you take incompatible mixtures, there will be fermentation in the stomach and intestines. All cereals can be taken with milk, fruits and vegetables. Do not take milk with milk-products—such as Rabdis, Peda, Kalakand, etc. Nuts, bread, apples, lemons, whey, butter, can be taken with everything. Proteins and starches, fruits and cereals or other carbohydrates are compatible combinations. Experience and instinct will guide you in making compatible mixtures of diets.

## DIETETIC PRINCIPLES

10. Do not eat when you are angry. Rest for a while till the mind becomes calm and then take your food. Poisons are secreted by the glands when you are angry and thrown into the blood stream.

11. Take food as medicine. Give up gluttony.

12. Do not eat anything between meals. Do not drink between meals. Do not eat late at night.

13. Do not remove the skin of apples and carrots, because, the skin has valuable minerals and vitamins.

14. Do not take tinned foods and old butter. Vegetables and rice should be steamed. Overcooking will rob the vegetables of their value and flavour. Do not throw away the water in which rice and vegetables are boiled. They contain valuable materials. Drink it also.

15. Take food at fixed hours. Take only two meals. Never heat the food again over the fire. Do not take too many dishes.

16. Sit on Vajrasana for 10 minutes after meals. This will digest your food well.

17. Take food when the breath is passing through the right nostril.

18. Make a change in your diet gradually. If an article of diet disagrees, reduce the quantity. It will be agreeable to you.

19. Observe silence when you take your food.

20. Protect the articles of diet from flies. Keep the milk in a cool place.

21. Do not do any strenuous work, physical or mental after taking food. Take rest for half an hour. Do not run immediately after food to catch the train.

22. Remember God, the Indweller in all foods, fruits and vegetables, the bestower of bounties to you during meals and at all times. Pray to Him just before and after meals.

## ARTICLES OF FOOD

### I

1. Apples contain vitamin A, B, and C, copper, potash, iron, phosphorus and malic acid. They serve the purpose of food.

2. Banana is rich in protein carbohydrate and vitamin B. Hence it serves almost as a food.

3. Buttermilk contains some calcium, phosphorus, iron and vitamin B-2.

4. Barley is rich in mineral matters.

5. Cornflour contains a high percentage of starch. It is prepared from maize.

6. Cereals constitute the most important of our vegetable foods. They are particularly rich in starch. They have very little fat. They contain protein.

7. Cheese is rich in vitamin A. It contains protein, fat, carbohydrate, calcium, phosphorus and iron.

8. Cabbage contains vitamin A, B, C, sulphur, calcium, phosphorus, iron, sodium and potassium. It is rich in vitamin C.

9. Carrot is very rich in vitamins A and C, lime, phosphorus, iron and potash.

10. Cocoanut contains protein, fat, carbohydrate, some vitamin A. No vitamin C. It is moderately rich in vitamin B. It contains calcium, phosphorus and iron.

11. Figs contain vitamin B, potash, sodium, lime, phosphorus and magnesium.

12. Fruits and vegetables are very valuable food-stuffs. They are protective foods.

13. Fruits and vegetables are very good sources of vitamins and minerals.

14. Groundnut contains protein of high quality. It contains good lecithin. It is equal to egg-yolk in this respect.

15. Grapes contain citric and tartaric acids.

16. Grapes, tomatoes, the leaves of green vegetables such as lettuce, cabbage, spinach are valuable sources of iron.

17. If you eat green leafy vegetables you can maintain perfect health even without milk.

18. Lettuce contains iron, phosphorus, lime, potash, and vitamins A, B and C.

19. Lemon contains plenty of vitamin C. It contains lime, phosphorus, potash, magnesium.

20. Molasses (gud) are rich in iron and carbohydrates.

21. Milk is the richest source of calcium. Cheese is next.

22. Milk and butter contain vitamin D.

23. Mango is a very potent source of vitamins A and C.

24. Nuts have very much nutritive value, though they are not very easy to digest. They form a valuable meat-substitute in the diet of vegetarians.

25. Nuts are rich in protein and fat. They are rich in vitamin B.

26. Oranges contain plenty of Vitamin C. They contain protein, fat, calcium, phosphorus and iron.

27. Potato is not rich in protein. It is a good source of vitamin C. It contains vitamins A, B, and B-2.

28. Pistacheo nuts (pista) contain proteins, fat, carbohydrates, calcium, phosphorus and iron.

29. Peanuts contain protein, fat, carbohydrates, calcium phosphorus, iron, vitamins A and B.

30. Pulses are the cheapest sources of protein. They can replace meat in the diet. They are most nutritious.

31. Polished rice is very rich in starch, but poor in fat and mineral.

32. Roots and tubers contain no protein or fat.

33. Red palm oil alone contains vitamin. Vegetable oils do not contain vitamins.

34. Root vegetables like potato are a good source of carbohydrates.

35. Spinach contains large amount of vitamins and calcium. It is rich in iron.

36. Skimmed milk contains calcium, phosphorus and iron.

37. Sweet potatoes are rich in Vitamin A. They contain vitamins B and C also.

38. Turnip contains iron, soda, potash, magnesium.

39. Tomato contains little protein and fat. It contains calcium, phosphorus, iron, vitamins A, B and C.

40. Walnuts contain calcium, phosphorus, iron, fat, protein, carbohydrates, vitamins A and B.

## II

1. Apple is useful in 'stones' in the kidneys or bladder.

2. Dates contain more iron than meat.

3. Fresh foods and cereals tend to form acid in the body. Vegetables and fruits with certain exceptions tend to form alkali.

4. Eat curry of plantain stem. This will dissolve stones in the kidneys and the bladder.

5. Pears are beneficial in stones in the bladder or kidneys. The stone will be dissolved.

## Chapter VI

### CARE OF THE EYES

Throughout the ages poets and philosophers have called the eyes "the mirrors in which the soul is reflected" and "windows of the mind". If words can hide one's true feelings, the expression in the eyes reveals to those who can read the state of mind of the speaker. To the medical world, the eye is much more than the organ of sight only, for through an examination of the fundus, many diseases of the body can be diagnosed. Indeed, no examination of the body is complete without the examination of the fundus.

Among the precious gifts God has bestowed upon mankind, eye-sight is certainly the foremost; for with its help we are able to appreciate and admire the beauty of nature, to express in silent speech more than any number of words can do what we feel. The eyes enable us to study the scriptures and through them to imbibe a knowledge of God. They are the lights that enable us to have the Darshan of Mahatmas, saints and sages. We adore the Murtis and pictures of the Lord, because we are able to SEE them! A pair of sound eyes makes life so much easier for man, and only the short-sighted would fail to take the utmost care of their eyes. And yet we find them, and their number is great. The reason may be ignorance or a lack of knowledge of hygienic principles—but the fact remains that India has comparatively more blind than any other country in the world, and the noteworthy feature of this is that more than 50% of all this blindness is preventable.

### BLINDNESS AND ITS CAUSES

Yet, we find that the number of people who fail to realise the importance of taking the utmost care of these two precious light centres, is great! The blind man not only leads a miserable life himself, but is a burden on others.

India has relatively more blind men than any other country in the world.

50% of all this blindness is preventable.

*Etiology of Blindness:* The factors causing blindness give rise to different rates of incidence at different ages. In infants, ophthalmia neonatorum is responsible for 50% of blindness, congenital abnormalities for 30% and other causes for the rest. Interstial keratitis, optic atrophy and ophthalmia neonatorum are the commonest causes in the school-going age. In adults choroiditis, optic atrophy, iridocyclitis and glaucoma are the commonest aetiological factors.

Syphilis, congenital as well as acquired, is responsible for blindness in a large number of cases.

Other common causes of blindness are infectious fevers, e.g., measles, smallpox; and local diseases of the eye, e.g., trachoma and high myopia. Injuries to the eyeball, accidental or those inflicted during war, are also factors that cause blindness.

Most of the causes of blindness are preventable.

## ANATOMY OF THE EYE

Nature has protected the eyes by keeping them in two sockets (orbital cavity), and further security is provided by the two eye-lids. The blinking reflex protects the eyes from any foreign body gaining entrance into them. In case a foreign body enters, tear glands which lie beneath the upper lids start secreting tears which wash down the intrusion. The eye-lashes and eye-brows act as barriers to particles of dust and insects, which would otherwise have gained easy entry into the eyes.

The front part of the eye is like a watch. The transparent glass covering the dial of the watch corresponds to the cornea, the anterior chamber which is filled with a watery fluid; the aqueous humour is like the space between the watch glass and the dial; the iris itself which may be of a green blue or brown colour is like the dial of the watch and has a central aperture, the pupil.

The pupil is comparable to the diaphragm of a camera which contracts in bright light and dilates in darkness. If a bright light is thrown on one eye, the pupils of both eyes contract. Behind the pupil lies the crystalline lens of plus 10D strength, which is held in place by the suspensory ligaments. The whole of the front part of the eye is covered by a transparent membrane, the conjunctiva, which is then reflected on to the inner part of the eye-lids.

The back part of the globe is lined by three membranes, which are the sclera (white portion), and choroid (pigmented) layers and the retina which is responsible for the reception of all visual impressions, which are then carried on to the brain through the optic nerve which enters the globe at its back part. Inside these membranes is a gelatinous fluid, the vitreous.

## CARE OF THE EYES

The eye may be affected in the course of general diseases of the body, e.g., acute infectious fevers like smallpox, or it may be affected by local diseases, e.g., myopia, trachoma. "Prevention is better than cure"; and this is particularly true of the diseases of the eye. If you follow the instructions outlined in the following pages, you will be able to keep your eyes very healthy and to have a good vision till the end of your life.

When reading, writing or sewing, too strong a light is as great an evil as one too dim; whether natural or artificial, the light should come from the left. It should never fall full in the face, but upon the work.

Daylight is the best when not shifted through curtains, and artificial light should be clear, steady, soft and white. The craze for coloured lamp shades has injured many eyes.

The eyes should never be steadily employed by artificial light, especially after a hard day's use; and to strain them in fading twilight, or by reading in cars or trains is an injurious practice.

*Illumination:* A normal eye can adapt itself to a wide range of intensity and quality of illumination. For ordinary work, an intensity of 5-20 candle power of light is desirable upon the object of study. Higher illumination is required for very fine work and for reading very fine type. Too bright illumination on the object is undesirable, because of the glare which will affect the eyes adversely. Thus, the practice of reading in the day so that the sunlight falls directly on the book must be avoided. If you must study in sunlight, assume such a position that your shadow falls on the object of study and your eyes are protected from direct light. Very harsh and contrasty marked shadows are undesirable. Soft shadows which can easily be obtained in the day by indirect illumination, e.g., by sitting in a well-ventilated room, are very good for the purpose of study. Undoubtedly, daylight is the best light for study. Reading in the shadow of a tree which has a thin shade, i.e., where shaded spots are freely mixed with bright spots, must be avoided. The light should emanate from a non-flickering source. The best light on a working desk, next to diffused indirect day-light, is a lamp which throws its lights on the book, leaving the eyes in shade. This light should be placed opposite and on the left side of the reader. It is a wise plan to keep the desk in the room in such a position that the daylight comes from the left.

Similarly, working in a poor light, e.g., bright moonlight or candle light, or studying by the fireside, causes a lot of strain on the eyes, and consequent damage to the eyes.

Illuminations recommended by Parsons for work, are above 50 C.P., for precision work to a high degree of accuracy, tasks requiring rapid discrimination (It has been experimentally proved now that discrimination is maximum with yellow light):

15-25 C.P. for prolonged critical visual tasks, e.g., proofreading, fine assembling and fine machine work.

10-15 C.P. for sustained reading and sewing on light goods.

Many modern artificial illuminators emit ultra-violet rays of light which are injurious to the eyes. But as most of such rays are absorbed by the glass covering the lamp, they do not affect the eyes much.

On a hot and sunny summer day, or during a dust-storm, do not move out unless you have protected your eyes with suitable goggles. Similarly, never carry a baby in bright sunlight unless you have shaded the eyes with a clean piece of cloth or an umbrella.

Studying in a reclining pose is injurious to the eyes; the venous return of blood is hindered, resulting in venous congestion and consequent eye strain. Reading immediately after

# CARE OF THE EYES

meals should be avoided as at that time more blood is directed to the digestive system, and reading then may upset your digestion. Take rest for at least 15 minutes after meals, before you restart your work.

The output of work done during the morning hours is much more than that obtained by working late hours at night.

The object of study should be placed at a distance of 15 inches from the eyes. Children who are myopic have a tendency to keep their books at a closer range. If you find this tendency in your child, or when the child complains of head-ache after studying for a while, or gets watering from the eyes after a little close work, have it examined for myopia, and get suitable glasses to correct the defect in the eye.

The common belief that wearing of glasses further weakens the eye-sight is entirely baseless. On the contrary, permanent damage may be done to the eyes of high myopes who persist in working without the use of suitable glasses.

It is essential to get the eyes examined by a good doctor, and suitable glasses taken. Only the best quality of lens must be used. Highly myopic children must wear the glasses constantly during the day, otherwise they will lose interest in the surroundings.

The lenses of the spectacles must be kept scrupulously clean and free from all traces of grease and dust. Clean the glasses several times a day. Never lift the glasses with your thumb or finger on the lenses. The spectacles must be taken off when you go to bed and kept in a good case to prevent breakage. The lenses must be carefully guarded against any scratches, since scratched lenses affect the eyes adversely. Whenever you want to place your glasses on a table, you should keep them in such a way that the lenses do not come in direct contact with the surface on which the glasses are placed. This can be done by keeping the glasses in such a way that the rims and the frame rest on the surface.

Glasses have their drawbacks. Some people do not like glasses for aesthetic reasons, and there is always the risk of the glasses falling off and getting broken. A new method (the contact-lens method) was suggested in 1827 by the well-known astronomer Sir John Herschel, but the technique was not perfected until recently. According to this new method, the lenses are worn in close contact with sclera; this provides a new optically perfect anterior chamber for the cornea without actually coming in contact with it. Thus it does not gives any discomfort to the patient. The space between the cornea and the lens is filled with a fluid allied to tears.

The fashioning and fitting of lenses requires a great deal of skill, since an ill-fitting lens will do more harm than good to the eyes.

There are several advantages in the contact-lens method:

(1) It forms part of the eye; therefore it can be used by persons who do not like to wear glasses.

(2) It may be used during sports, while swimming, playing tennis or cricket or riding, without any risk of the lens falling and breaking.

(3) The vision is unrestricted.

(4) In certain diseases of the eye, e.g., keratoconus, where glasses are absolutely useless, these lenses often give miraculous results.

The most important limitation in the case of contact-lenses was the fogging of vision after six to eight hours of using the lenses, due to the accumulation between the cornea and the lens of carbon dioxide thrown out by the cornea. This has, however, been overcome by the provision of ventilation holes in the lens.

(5) Intermittent rest is essential during a prolonged period of study. In this interval you should keep on blinking regularly. Blinking reflex is a device of Nature to give rest and protection to the eye. By the process of blinking, the eyes are kept moist, and all particles of dust and products of excretion from the eyes are washed away. The process of blinking should be frequent and effortless. Blink frequently, if you want your eyes to be healthy.

(6) After a period of study for an hour or two, close your eyes, relax for a while and repeat your Ishta Mantra. Or, you may get up and walk for a few minutes. This will give rest to your eyes and keep you refreshed. Some people can work much better

## CARE OF THE EYES

if after four or five hours of work they have a short nap for fifteen minutes.

(7) Studying while travelling in a motor vehicle or a tonga causes a lot of eye-strain and headache, since the movement and jerks of the vehicle do not allow proper fixation of the words, and consequently it takes a greater effort to read the words.

(8) It is a bad practice to read when you are suffering from some acute fever or immediately after convalescence, as during these periods much more strain is put on the eyes and brain. Such practice may lead to permanent damage to the eyes.

(9) During the planning of a house, special attention must be paid to the kitchen, which must be well-ventilated and so constructed that the room does not get smoky during cooking, since smoke is very injurious to the eyes.

(10) You will often notice that children are very keen on looking at new surroundings while travelling in a train, and consequently they will look towards the direction in which the train in moving. This is a dangerous practice, since by so doing particles of coal-dust or little pieces of stone will fall into the eyes and injure them.

(11) The choice of toys for children requires a careful selection. It is inadvisable to present children with toys like bow and arrow, darts, air-guns, toy-pistols, scissors or knives by which they may accidentally injure their own eyes or the eyes of their young friends. Some children are very fretful and will hit their parents with anything they have in their hands and may thus injure their (the parents') eyes. In such cases, it is wrong to get irritated and scold them. On the contrary, a careful psychological approach must be made and their attention diverted to something useful. Parents should study child psychology. Toys like meccano help develop the brains of children and are good gifts to be made to the proud mothers of these innocent souls. (See the Maria Montessori method).

(12) It is the duty of mill-owners, especially those running iron and cement factories to provide suitable goggles and other forms of protection to their workers, to prevent foreign bodies from flying into the eyes. In case an eye is injured accidentally,

immediate attention by an ophthalmic surgeon must be arranged; otherwise even the other eye might be endangered due to what is known as 'sympathetic Ophthalmia'.

(13) In India most of the deliveries of pregnant women are conducted by untrained nurses who are absolutely ignorant of one of the greatest causes of blindness—ophthalmic neonatorum. The disease is caused by gonorrhoea in the mother. The eyes of the child do not secret any tears during the first week after the birth of the child. Any watery or purulent secretion from the eyes of the child during the first week must be taken as an indication of this disease—ophthalmic neonatorum. At that stage, if proper treatment is given, the disease is easily curable. When the eyes of the child after birth are still closed, the nurse should thoroughly clean and dry the eyelids of the child. The eyes are then opened and a drop of 1% silver nitrate instilled into each eye. The use of penicillin ophthalmic ointment regularly during the first week of birth is again very helpful and absolutely safe.

Once the disease is detected, an eye-specialist must be consulted immediately and advice taken from him for the prevention of the disease from spreading to the other members of the family.

(14) Certain drugs may set up inflammation of the optic nerve of the eye leading to blindness, methyl alcohol being an important example. Alcohol and its allied intoxicating drinks must, therefore, be refrained from as much as possible. Some drunkards even drink methylated spirit if alcohol is not available. This practice is extremely dangerous since it may lead to permanent blindness. Lead and Arsenic are other drugs which require careful handling. Arsenic is very often administered by quacks. These even when administered by physicians without due care sometimes may lead to blindness.

(15) Not only has the careless pleasure-seeker to pay a heavy penalty for the sense-gratification, but even his offsprings may suffer the consequences of his loose behaviour. His children may be born blind due to ophthalmic neonatorum, or lose their vision when they are in their full bloom of youth as a result of interstitial keratitis. If a man suffers from venereal diseases, he

## CARE OF THE EYES

must get himself properly treated. Mothers who have suffered from syphilis must take a course of anti-syphilitic drugs during each pregnancy.

(16) A healthy eye does not require any lotions or eye-drops. These are not only superfluous, but actually undesirable, unless there is some definite indication for their use. It is a good practice to bathe your eyes regularly with good, clean, cold and sprinkling water. This will increase their resistance against disease and will preserve the vision. In case you suffer from a mild inflammatory reaction in your eye, resort may be had to penicillin eye ointment, cibazol eye ointment, or the instillation of 5% solution of argyrol or 5% protorgal solution after thoroughly cleansing the eyes with a weak warm boric lotion several times in a day. Hot boric fomentations are especially very valuable in most inflammatory disorders of the eyes. Another safe and very useful alternative is the instillation of penicillin drops made up of a strength so that 1 cc of water contains 10,000 units or 20,000 units of the *antibiotic*. The solution can be easily prepared by adding 10 cc or 5 cc of distilled water, respectively, to a bottle of penicillin containing 100,000 units of crystalline penicillin. The drops should be put at half-hourly intervals for the first three hours and then every hour. It is important to bear in mind the fact that the penicillin solution is quite unstable and that, once it is mixed with water, penicillin loses its potency after 4-5 days, even when kept under proper storage conditions. Penicillin eye ointment, however, is quite stable and must be used within the period of the last date prescribed. Penicillin drops are very efficacious against ophthalmic neonatorum, too.

(17) Every member of the family must have his own towel, and mothers should so deeply instil this idea in the minds of their children that they never use each other's towels and handkerchiefs, since this is a very common mode of spreading of diseases of the eye.

(18) It is a well-known fact, if a man falls ill and he wants to get well early, he must take a good rest. Your delicate eye is no exception to the rule. Whenever you have some eye trouble, you must give adequate rest to your eyes. Just as sick horses, if they

are whipped, will keep on running for sometime, after which they will completely collapse, your eyes when put cruelly to work, will ultimately break down completely.

(19) *Presbyopia:* After the age of 35, the eye must be regularly examined because after this age plus-lenses have generally to be used for reading work, even though the eyes are otherwise healthy.

## DIET

Good, well-balanced, diet is absolutely essential, not only for maintaining a good standard of health, but also for preserving the health of the eyes. Hence, the importance of selecting food-stuffs which include all the essentials of a balanced diet. The deficiency of any one of the factors of the balanced diet may lead to serious results. Thus, the deficiency of Vitamin in diet may lead to serious results. Thus, the deficiency of Vitamin A in diet leads to night blindness and a host of general diseases of the body and local diseases of the eye.

In some good hotels in U.S.A., the menu card indicates the diet-value of all the dishes which are served in the hotel. They also provide a chart in which the details of dietetic requirements for individuals of different occupations are given. This is a good practice, which may be adopted in this country also.

Food should consist of proteins, fats, carbohydrates, salts, water, vitamins and some amount of roughage to stimulate intestinal peristalsis. No single food-stuff contains all these in a balanced proportion, though milk is the nearest approach to it.

Proteins (also known as nitrogenous or flesh-forming substances) are most essential for the maintenance of life and growth of the body. All proteins do not have the same food value, the latter depending upon the amino-acid content of the protein. Proteins are of two types (a) superior proteins which include milk and animal proteins; (b) inferior proteins of corn, wheat and beans. Vegetable proteins cannot entirely replace animal proteins, as some of the amino-acids, e.g., lysin, cystin, tryptophane and tyrosin, which are essential for growth, are lacking in them. At least one-third of the protein that we take should be derived from animal-source. Milk contains all the amino-acid essential to the growth of the body.

The requirement of proteins is increased during growth, during pregnancy and convalescence after prolonged fevers. Daily requirement of proteins is one gram per kilo of body-weight, more than which should not be consumed.

*Fats:* "Protein sparing food" yields 2¼ times as much energy as an equal weight of proteins or carbohydrates. Fats produce great heat and hence are used in excess in colder climates. Fats are very rich in Vitamins A and D. Vegetable oils, however, lack vitamins. 50-100 grammes of fat is daily required for an adult person.

*Carbohydrates:* These are found in cane sugar, glucose, starch, cereals, etc. Each gram of sugar yields 4.1 calories of heat.

Mineral salts form one-twentieth of the body weight and include calcium, potassium, sodium, iron, copper, manganese, magnesium, phosphorus, sulphur, chlorine and iodine.

Phosphorus is essential for multiplication of cells, and its deficiency leads to softening of bones, stunted growth, poor bone formations, caries of teeth, etc. Foods rich in phosphorus are oatmeal, almonds, pear, beans, whole wheat, milk, spinach, etc.

Calcium is essential for clotting of blood, rhythmic action of the heart and development of bones. Its chief source is milk. Rice is very poor in calcium content. Increased intake of calcium is essential during the period of growth, pregnancy and lactation. Much of the calcium is lost during cooking, e.g., milk on boiling loses much of its calcium and the scum takes up and retains the calcium phosphate.

Iron is essential for the formation of red blood cells. 6-12 milligram of this is needed every day. It is found in pulses, whole cereals, grains, dates, figs, raisins, etc. The iron found in cereals and pulses is more assimilative than that found in vegetables.

Iodine is found in goat's milk and fresh vegetables and in very minute quantities in drinking water. Its deficiency leads to goitre. Its intake should be increased during lactation, pregnancy and growing period.

Vitamins exist in foods in minute quantities and their deficiencies may even lead to death. There are water-soluble and fat-soluble vitamins. Water-soluble vitamins are Vitamin B-complex, C and P. Fat-soluble Vitamins are A, D, E and K. Vitamins can be synthesised by plants, but not by animal bodies.

Vitamin A is found in abundance in cream, butter, carrots, cabbage, etc. Milk does not lose this vitamin by boiling or pasteurising, but when evaporated by vacuum or aeration, it is destroyed. Its deficiency retards growth and lowers resistance to general and local infection; and causes xerophthalmia and night-blindness. Various types of paralysis may develop. Daily requirement 4000-6000 units. This Vitamin prevents infections, especially against infections of respiratory passages.

*Vitamin B-complex:* It has several constituents, the important ones being (1) Thiamine hydrochlor or B-1. Vitamin B, Source: Rice polishings, yeast. Its deficiency leads to beri-beri. (2) Riboflavin. This has been isolated from milk. Its deficiency in animals causes cataract and degeneration of nerves. Deficiency of Nicotinic acid leads to pellagra.

*Vitamin C:* Ascorbic acid, cevetamic acid. Source: cabbage, turnips, lemons, oranges, germinating barley and green vegetables. Amla is very rich in Vitamin C. Heating and drying destroy this Vitamin; Amla is an exception to this rule. The Vitamin C content of milk is very variable and increases during summer when the cattle graze on green grass. Mother's milk contains Vitamin C sufficient for the baby's requirement till he is six months old, beyond which age this has to be supplemented with other foods. It is essential, therefore, to supplement the baby's diet, after that age, with fresh juice of citrus fruits, e.g., oranges and malta, or with tomato juice. A very cheap and rich source of Vitamin C can be obtained as follows:

Put some dry grams on a jute bag soaked in water, and cover it with a rug again drenched with water. Keep it overnight in the open. In one or two days, young sprouts will spring out of the grams. The grams thus prepared have been found to have a very high Vitamin C content and are very nourishing.

It is important to bear in mind the fact that Vitamin C is destroyed at a temperature of 100 degree C. Thus, most of the food-value of tomatoes is wasted during the process of cooking or frying.

Deficiency of this constituent of diet leads to defective maturation of red blood cells and is thus responsible for certain types of anaemia, loss of weight, dental caries, scurvy characterised by bleeding and spongy gums and some haemorrhagic diseases.

Some physicians have advocated high doses of Vitamin C for frequent attacks of cold and claim that, if this is given in high doses, it will avert the attack or cut it short. This Vitamin inhibits the growth of several micro-organisms and is, therefore, a necessary factor for resisting infection.

Daily human requirement of Vitamin C is 50-100 mgms. A pint of boiled milk contains about 5 mgms; fresh raw milk contains 14 mgms. Fresh orange juice contains 50 mgms per 100 cc of the juice.

Vitamin P occurs naturally with Vitamin C. Its deficiency can lead to haemoptysis and may affect the lungs giving rise to symptoms of tuberculosis.

*Calciferol-Vitamin D:* This Vitamin is an essential factor for the proper development of bones and so prevents rickets. This Vitamin can be produced in the body when one sits in sunlight. This is found in high concentrations in cod-liver oils. Vitamin D content of cow's milk can be enriched by irradiation to sunlight. Vitamin D is essential for the absorption of calcium. The administration of calcium in high doses without corresponding provision of Vitamin D in diet or otherwise, is, therefore, useless.

Vitamin E is more stable to heat than Vitamin A. Anti-sterility Vitamin E, when given in high doses to women who do not bear children, helps conception. High doses of this vitamin have recently been used for rheumatic heart and have given very encouraging results. It is found in the embryo of seeds and in green leaves, especially cotton seed, maize, peas, oats and lettuce.

Vitamin K: Its absence prevents blood from coagulating, and thus a wound will keep on bleeding for long periods. It is found in alfalfa grass.

Folic acid is another factor recently isolated, and has proved very good for certain types of anaemias.

Water is most essential for the maintenance of life of animals and vegetables. You must drink large quantities of fresh pure sparkling water obtained from a good source.

Daily requirement of diet for an individual has to be determined after taking into consideration the weight, sex, age, height, occupation of the person, and the season, climate, etc,

An average man requires 2500-3500 calories. During growth, pregnancy and lactation, dietary requirement is increased. Old people and women require less food than young men.

A mixed diet is easily digestible. The food should be well cooked, tasty and palatable, not because it is simply a gratification for your sense of taste, because delicious food stimulates the secretion of digestive juices.

Taking in of plenty of roughage will cure even cases of chronic constipation.

Milk is the only food which approaches the "Perfect Food". Consume a lot of milk and milk products and do not get addicted to tea, coffee and cocoa, which are habit-forming and have little or no food value.

## CONJUNCTIVITIS

There are several varieties of conjunctivitis. The disease affects all ages, children as well as adults. The symptoms of this disease are a sense of discomfort, described as grittiness, inability to keep the eyes open, variable amount of watery, muco-purulent discharge from the eyes. The child is afraid of opening its eyes in the light. The eyes are red and very much swollen.

*Treatment:* Remove the cause. If due to infection, clean the eyes, remove all traces of discharge and instil 2 drops of 5% argyrol or progorgal three times a day. Another alternative is the use of penicillin ointment ophthalmic. Instead, penicillin drops with a strength of 1 cc having 10,000 units may be instilled half-hourly for three hours and then every hourly. This method of treatment is very useful and it is advisable to supplement it with hot fomentation. The eyes must be washed several times a day with warm boric lotion. The use of tinted glasses, e.g., crooks, while going out in the sun, is advisable. More serious cases should be kept under the care of a good ophthalmologist.

## CATARACT

Cataract is very common in India and chiefly a disease of old age. Young people, however, are not infrequently affected.

Diabetes is a great predisposing cause. Many cases are congenital.

Appearance of stationary black spots in front of eyes is usually the first symptom. Many patients see better in a dull light than in a bright; in some varieties of the disease, the reverse is the case. When the cataract gets mature, the patient cannot "count fingers", but can just feel light vaguely and can find out the direction from which the light is coming. It will be interesting to note that if a torchlight is focussed on an eye with an immature cataract, a shadow of the iris will be found on the lens. Whereas in the case of mature cataract, no shadow of the iris is visible on the lens. When this stage has been reached, the eye is fit for operation. The rate of maturation (of the lens) is very variable; some patients lose their vision completely within one year, while in other cases the cataract will not mature for 12 years.

The operation is done under a local anaesthesia and is absolutely painless; and of a short duration. Great asepsis must be observed, and perfect rest is advisable on the first day. If before the disease started the patient had no refractive error, he will get full vision after the operation.

## GLAUCOMA

This may come on suddenly or in an insidious fashion. In an acute attack, intense pain is felt over the affected eye and temple, and vomiting may also be caused. This is accompanied by great constitutional disturbance, and the vision suddenly decreases, so that within a few hours it may be reduced to merely counting of fingers or complete blindness. Generally, however, the condition improves and the loss of vision depends on the severity of the attack,—it may be very mild or very severe; in the former case, the resultant damage is slight, and may be great in the latter case.

Instillation of eserine 1% in the affected eye alongwith analgesics should be the line of treatment adopted. As soon as the attack comes on, a doctor should be consulted. Some sort of operation, after the acute phase has passed off, is generally necessary.

In the chronic non-congestive type of the disease, the onset of the disease is very insidious and can only be diagnosed by a physician.

Corneal opacities occur often as a result of injury or corneal ulceration, the latter being secondary to trachoma or the constant friction of inturned eye-lashes rubbing against the cornea. The ulcer on healing gives rise to opacities of various grades depending on the depth of the ulcer.

The treatment consists of tattooing the white spot; thus, good cosmetic results can be obtained.

Corneal transplantation by operation is also done by choice. Square corneal transplant is taken from the healthy eye of a stillborn child or the eye of a person immediately after death and stitched on to the eye under operation. The healthy cornea of an eye which had to be taken out due to some disease is also used. A square piece of cornea going to the depth of the whole opacity is removed from the eye under operation before the transplant is stitched. The whole procedure takes 10-14 days and gives very encouraging results.

When vision is interfered with, in the case of a central opacity, the eye-sight can be restored by a very minor and painless operation.

## ERRORS OF REFRACTION

*Myopia or short-sightedness.* The patient cannot see distant objects clearly. High myopia causes discomfort after near work and black spots may be found floating in front of the eyes. Patient keeps the book very near his eyes during study.

Treatment consists in wearing suitable glasses which must be worn constantly.

Myopes should not do close work for long duration. The book must be placed at a distance of 15 inches from the eyes. All instructions given already in this section must be strictly adhered to. The books intended for children must be printed in big, bold letters. Myopic children are usually very intelligent and fond of studies, and therefore their study hours must be carefully regulated.

For high myopes, some operation may have to be done under the care of an expert surgeon.

Hypermetropia or far-sightedness may not reveal any symptoms. Some symptoms are noticeable, however, after study by artificial illumination. A sense of discomfort or undue dryness in the eye may be present, causing frequent blinking. If the work is continued, patient gets headache on the forehead or on one side of the head.

There is no need for treatment, unless there is some complaint, in which case suitable lenses must be used.

*Presbyopia.* After the age of 40, due to certain physiological changes in the lens, a person has to keep the book at a longer distance than usual, to see the letters clearly. Every 5 years after 40, increase of approximately plus ID strength or a little less is required and consequently a suitable plus lens should be taken from an ophthalmologist if any feeling of discomfort is felt.

## EYE-SIGHT OF INDIANS

The average eye-sight of an Indian is generally not more powerful than a European's, but certainly less than that of some Nomadic tribes, for example the Nubians. The strong sun-glare in the tropical regions has a somewhat injurious effect on the vision. But the Native population of India possesses a hereditary disposition to endure the glare of strong light without much harm. In spite of this, eye-diseases are more prevalent among

Indians than among Europeans. It is due to deficiency of vitamins or, in other words, insufficient vitality in parts and in total. The most common of these diseases are scrofulous eye-affections.

The cause of old-age cataract forming in Indians is lack of constitutional energy. Extremely weak organic resistance is also answerable for the great number of cases and detachment of the retina and for the frequent occurrence of glaucoma, which often leads to blindness due to increased tension. Myopia is found more among the literate classes. It is rarely found among the peasants who are free from much eye-straining work. A child blessed with excellent eye-sight at the time it enters school life may become short-sighted due to over-straining of the eye, reading in highly powerful or dim light exactly by the same manner as does a European child under similar conditions. Colour-blindness is almost non-existent among Indians.

Scorfulous affections of the eye, such as phylactenular, can be greatly minimised by improving hygienic conditions. Modern living, in spite of its numerous comforts, has a degenerating effect on the Nation's health. You must go back to Nature if you wish to live a happy, disease-free life. Unnatural means and artificial restoratives should be avoided as far as possible. All should possess a general knowledge of the vitamins contained in the food articles and their usefulness to the body. Eyes should be protected from the dust and washed with cool water as many times as possible.

The eyes of the Indians are usually more lustrous than those of the Europeans. The sparkle is due to a reflex of light on the surface of the pupils. There is a larger opening of the eyelids, too. Hence the Indian's eyes appear to be large. Pupils by themselves are quite expressionless. But the surrounding muscles of the eye convey one's feelings and emotions.

There is a great future for the ophthalmic health of the Nation. Dietetic standard must be improved and proper knowledge of hygiene should be universally imparted.

# Chapter VII

## PHYSICAL CULTURE
### EXERCISE AND BREATHING

1. A life of ease, luxury and inactivity is detrimental to good health. Some form of exercise is absolutely essential to maintain and improve one's health and physique.

2. Exercise assists in a marked degree the free movements of the bowels and promotes regularity. Riding, rowing, running, swimming, cycling, badminton, tennis, Asanas, Suryanamaskara, Danda, Baithaks, gymnastics are beneficial.

3. Exercise causes profuse perspiration. This keeps the skin active and healthy. Exercise also helps to keep the blood clean and pure.

4. Be regular in your exercise. Be systematic. Do not fatigue yourself. If there is fatigue, you have gone beyond your capacity. Reduce the number of exercises and the period of exercise. There should be perfect exhilaration of spirit, after exercise. Do not go beyond your capacity. Infrequent, severe exercise is not very beneficial. It may do more harm than good.

5. Take sufficient exercise daily, stopping short of fatigue. There should be perfect exhilaration after exercise. If there is fatigue, you have gone beyond your capacity. Reduce the period of exercise.

6. Exercise and rest must be balanced, if you want to keep up good health.

7. Exercise and fresh air play the most important part in developing your physique.

8. Strength and size are not always the same. Either a thin or a wiry or a heavy-built man may be strong.

9. Weight remains more or less stationary between the ages 30 and 50. Then it slowly decreases as the energy decreases.

10. *Breathing:* The number of heart beats in a healthy adult

is 72 per minute. The number of breathing is 18 per minute. The ratio between breathing and heart beat is 1 : 4. The heart beats 4 times to each breath.

11. An adult breathes about 15 or 16 times in a minute, a woman 18, children breathe much more often. A pneumonia patient breaths 80, 100 or even 120 times per minute.

12. The dust contains countless disease-producing germs. Therefore remove the dust from your house. Do not inhale dust.

13. Breathing through the mouth is very harmful. Therefore do not breathe through the mouth.

14. Keep the mouth shut except when you have something to swallow or something good to say.

15. The air that you breathe into your lungs contains plenty of oxygen; but that which you breathe out contains very little of oxygen and is not fit to be breathed again.

16. Never cover the face with bed-sheets. You will injure the body by breathing over and over again the foul, poisonous, expired air.

17. Through perspiration many poisonous things, such as carbon dioxide, salts, etc., come out of the body. The skin is a respiratory organ also. If the skin were coated with some kind of paint or varnish so that the perspiration cannot escape, death will take place in a few hours.

18. Rub the body vigorously with a rough towel. This will open all the pores of the skin and cleanse the body properly.

19. The lungs can be developed through the practice of deep breathing exercises.

## REVITALISATION IN A FEW SECONDS
## BHASTRIKA

Pranayama is a great help to Sadhakas. It has innumerable advantages. The mind will be more easily concentrated during meditation if you sit after one or two rounds of Bhastrika. You can effectively drive off sleep and drowsiness during meditation with the help of this Pranayama. No tea or coffee is necessary. Lungs get thoroughly exercised and flushed. The Pranayama is a sure remedy for Asthma. It increases the gastric fire. too. Digestion is improved. In a few moments the entire body and mind are revitalised. In cold places, even if you have no blankets, practise vigorous Bhastrika. You will be comfortable. The Pranayama will produce warmth in the body. Padmasana is the best Asana for practising Bhastrika and Kapalabhati.

This is very much like Kapalabhati. In Kapalabhati, breathing is automatically controlled by the pressure and relaxation of abdominal muscles. When the belly is drawn in, the diaphragm is thrown up and the lungs will automatically throw out the breath: similarly, when the abdominal pressure is relaxed, the diaphragm will descend, thus creating a vaccum in the lungs, and automatically the breath is taken in. There is no particular attention paid to breathing and hence it is more a diaphragmatic exercise. But, in Bhastrika, besides the abdominal muscles, attention is paid to breathing also. Forced expulsion of breath characterises this Pranayama. The nostrils and the entire bronchial tube as also the lungs are vigorously cleansed. Here special attention is paid to Rechaka alone. Puraka becomes an inevitable corollary. Puraka should be mild, short and automatic, and just that much of breath should be taken in as would be sufficient for the next forcible expulsion. At the end Bhastrika has a long, mild and full Puraka, followed by a long Kumbhaka and then a full Rechaka. In Bhastrika the maximum number of expulsions per round is 20 and a Sadhaka is advised to do only three rounds per sitting. There should be a clear interval between two rounds. In Kapalabhati the expulsions can go up to a maximum of 100 at a time.

All of you should make it a point, whenever you meet an Asthmatic, to teach this Pranayama (Bhastrika) to him. You will be rendering a great service. You should teach this Pranayama to all those with whom you come in contact.

## PHYSICAL CULTURE IN BED

There is a general misconception that physical culture is only for the youth that the more aged men and women should just helplessly watch old age set in. No. Even middle-aged people have benefited by a regular practice of Asanas and Pranayamas.

By gradual practice they can thoroughly master all the important Asanas and Pranayamas. Patience and perseverance are required. They can start with following simple exercises which they can do regularly in bed as soon as they get up in the morning. The entire series of exercises will not take up more than fifteen minutes; and these fifteen minutes will bestow on them greater fitness for the day's activities and longevity also.

Sit up in bed cross-legged.

### Exercise No. 1

Catch hold of your left ankle with your right hand, behind your back. Now bend forward and touch the ground with your forehead.

Release the hold on the left ankle and in one backward motion swing back, resting the two palms on the ground.

Keep the right palm on the ground and swing the trunk to the right and touch the ground on the right side with the left palm also.

Twist the trunk to the left side and place both the palms on the ground on the left side.

### Exercise No. 2

Stretch the legs forward.

Catch hold of the toes with your hands.

Try to bend forward and touch the knees with your forehead, without bending the knees.

### Exercise No. 3

Sit cross-legged again.

Breathe out completely and slowly. Draw the belly in (Uddiyana Bandha).

### Exercise No. 4

Release the abdomen. Breathe normally.

Now, draw the belly in and release in rapid succession. Do not hold the breath. Do not shake the body also violently. This is an exercise exclusively for the stomach. This is called Agnisara.

### Exercise No. 5

Close the fist and raise the forearm, bending at the elbows.

Throw the arms forward; then again draw the forearm backward, bending at the elbows. Repeat this three or four times.

Stretch the arms sideways, and resume the normal position.

Similarly, stretch the arms upwards and bring them back to the normal position.

### Exercise No. 6

*Bhastrika, slow:* Sit cross-legged. Now breathe in and out forcibly, drawing the belly in and out as in the case of bellows. At the end of a few rounds (say, six), take a deep breath, retain in as long as you can and breathe out.

*Bhastrika, quick:* The same process may be gone through more rapidly, the inhalations and exhalations following each other in rapid succession.

*Bhastrika, internal:* Close the glottis partially, so that, as you breathe in and out, the throat produces a hissing noise (instead of the nostrils producing the noise). The rest of the process is the same for the other form of Bhastrika.

*Kapalabhati* is similiar to Bhastrika. Here the inhalations and exhalations are rapid; there is no forced expulsions of breath as much as there is in Bhastrika. And, there is no retention at the end.

*Sitali:* Protrude the tongue little away from the lips. Fold the tongue like a tube. Draw in the air through the mouth with the hissing sound si, si, si. Retain the breath as long as you can hold on with comfort. Then exhale slowly through both nostrils. Practise this three or four times.

*Sitkari:* Fold the tongue so that the tip of the tongue might touch the upper palate and draw the air through the mouth with a hissing sound (si, si, si, si). Then retain the breath as long as you can without the feeling of suffocation and then exhale slowly through both nostrils. You can keep the two rows of teeth in contact and then inhale the air through the mouth as before.

## Exercise No. 7

Hold the head erect.

Roll the eye-balls up and down, then left and right. Then move the eye-balls from end to end, crosswise.

This can easily be done if you fix four points in front of you—one right above the top of your head, another near your feet, one on your right, and the other to your left. Look at this point without moving your head. Similarly the crosswise movement also.

Then move the eye-ball in a semi-circular movement. Start from the left corner, then, slowly roll it to the right corner, along the edge of that upper eye-lid. Similarly along the lower eye-lids also.

Complete this exercise by rotating the eye-balls in a circular moving, clockwise and anti-clockwise.

These few exercises in themselves are enough to keep you all healthy and to increase your longevity.

## SURYANAMASKARA TECHNIQUE

ॐ सूर्यं सुन्दरलोकनाथममृतं वेदान्तसारं शिवं
ज्ञानं ब्रह्ममयं सुरेशममलं लोकैकचित्तं स्वयम् ।
इन्द्रादित्यं नराधिपं सुरगुरुं त्रैलोक्य चूडामणिं
ब्रह्माविष्णुशिवस्वरूपहृदयं वन्दे सदा भास्करम् ॥

After repeating the above Surya Dhyana Sloka, uttering the Twelve Names of Surya, perform Suryanamaskara (one complete Namaskara after each name).

ॐ मित्राय नमः
ॐ रवये नमः
ॐ सूर्याय नमः
ॐ भानवे नमः
ॐ खगाय नमः

# SURYANAMASKARA TECHNIQUE

ॐ पूष्णे नमः
ॐ हिरण्यगर्भाय नमः
ॐ मरीचये नमः
ॐ आदित्याय नमः
ॐ सवित्रे नमः
ॐ अर्काय नमः
ॐ भास्कराय नमः

*Pose No. 1.* Stand erect with palms folded, in a prayerful attitude.

*Pose No. 2.* Raise the hands over the head. Hold the hands firm and erect.

*Pose No. 3.* Swing the hands forward and downward, along with the trunk. Keeping the knees straight, touch the ground with the palms. Let the palms rest alongside the feet. Bury the face between the knees in the manner of Padahasthasana.

*Pose No. 4.* Throw the right foot backward, at the same time bending the left foot at the knee. Raise the head and gaze at the sun or the sky. The left knee should be between the hands.

*Pose No. 5.* Take the left foot also backward. Let the head, trunk and legs form one straight line. The whole body will now rest on the toes and palms.

*Pose No. 6.* (Namaskara) Lower the body so that (1) the forehead, (2) the chest, (3-4) the two palms, (5-6) the two knees, and (7-8) the two feet alone touch the ground. This is Sashtanga Namaskara.

*Pose No. 7.* Raise the head slowly and bend the spine. Turn the face skyward, in the manner of Bhujangasana.

*Pose No. 8.* Swing the trunk backwards, keeping the palms on the ground. Let the heels also touch the ground. The whole body will assume the shape of an inverted U now.

*Pose No. 9.* Same as Pose No. 4.
*Pose No. 10.* Same as Pose No. 3.
*Pose No. 11.* Same as Pose No. 2.
*Pose No. 12.* Same as Pose No. 1.

## PHYSICAL CULTURE FOR BABIES

Give your four-week old infant "setting-up" exercises. Teach him to do the bicycle and to stand on his head. Strange as the idea may sound to some, it is very useful. A daily routine of callisthenics helps build a strong back and good posture and pays big dividends in health and energy. Any enterprising mother can easily give her youngster his daily workout. She does not need any special training. Just a certain amount of time and patience. And when things really get going, she will get as much fun out of baby's stunts as he does. Best place for the exercises is a warm well-ventilated room. Baby should not be wearing anything but a diaper. Be careful to pick a safe place for him to lie, with lots of room for rolling around. Right time for the daily dozen is just before the morning bath.

First of all comes bicycling. Put the baby on his back and grasp one tiny ankle in each hand. Then push and pull the tiny legs into a bicycling motion. Repeat a couple of times the first day, three times the second, and increase the number each day until he is doing it eight or ten times.

The next exercise is even simpler, and he will love it. Roll him over on his tummy, then on his back, then on to his tummy again. Repeat several times. In a short while you will find him rolling over without any assistance from you.

Next you are going to teach him to stand on his head—well, practically. Put him on his back and firmly grasp his ankles again. Lift him gently until he is resting on his shoulders. He will automatically stiffen his spine to brace himself. This is a strenuous exercise (like the Sarvangasana); so just let him do it a couple of times.

Then give him a little rest from all this hard work. Allow him a free kicking period. If you can put up with a little noise, he will do it best if he is allowed to kick the bed he is lying on. The thump, thump of his own small feet will please him mightily.

After this has gone on for a few minutes, you can get back to the serious business of exercises again. Put him on his back and persuade him to grasp a finger in each of your hands. Curl your fingers around his wrist as an extra precaution. Now, pull him up gently. Only his back will lift at first, but after a while, he will manage to pull up his head, allowing you to pull him into sitting position. Never attempt to force him. Wait until he indicates himself that he is ready to take this big step.

Put him on his back again. Grasp his ankle and gently flex his legs at the hip joint, knees straight until his toes come near his chest. Don't push down. Just go as far as his legs seem capable of bending comfortably. Return to the starting position.

A variation of this exercise is to grasp his ankles and to bring his knees down until they touch his abdomen.

The final exercise is very easy and one that baby will soon do by himself. Just raise his arms over his head and then down again to his sides.

After the exercises are over, he should go right into a nice warm tub followed by an oil rub down. Then by the time he has had his milk, he should be really ready to enjoy a good sleep.

A few minutes a day devoted to this daily dozen will mean increased vitality and strength for your child. Of course, you must be careful not to tire him, and the exercise should not be continued beyond the point of fatigue. You will find it pretty easy to judge by his own reactions as to just how he feels about it.

## MASSAGE AND HEALTH

1. Massage is methodical shampooing. It consists of rubbing, stroking, kneading, principally in the direction of the muscles.

2. Massage is rubbing and manipulating the body according to scientific rules, which strengthen the tissues. The different movements are stroking, kneading, rubbing or friction and percussion. Massage is an exercise for the patient.

3. It is a substitute for exercise. Skilled knowledge of a skilled masseur is highly beneficial.

4. Massage must be done gently, patiently and leisurely. It should not be done in a hurry.

5. Violent rubbing and manipulation by wrestlers and acrobats is strongly condemned.

6. All the movements—kneading, rubbing, beating and rolling—are made from the extremities towards the heart.

7. Bear in mind that pain must never be produced by massage. Always massage in the direction of venous return.

8. Massage before bath is invigorating. It should not be merely applying friction. It should be rubbing with a firm grip on the limbs. It should take the form of a kneading or pressing down movement on the muscles with closed fist.

9. Groundnut oil or cocoanut oil may be rubbed while massaging. This lubricates, cleanses and also feeds the patient. The patient can be exposed to the morning sun for 15 or 30 minutes.

10. Rub the abdomen all over for 10 minute every night and morning with a rough towel.

11. Massage stimulates the action of the skin and the blood-circulation. It soothes the nerves and removes muscular pain, etc.

12. It stimulates the skin muscles and superficial vessels. It promotes the flow of blood and lymph and the excretion of effete matter. Thus it excites appetite to supply the place of removed material.

13. Massage helps the absorption of inflammatory and effete products and the acceleration of the lymph flow, and relieves tension in muscles and other tissues. It restores the tone to muscles weakened by disuse or disease and relieves pain in the muscles and nerves.

14. Massage is useful in chronic inflammation of joints. It should not be given in diseases of the heart, gastric, ulcer and acute inflammation of joints.

## DAILY ELECTRIC MASSAGE

Get a small hand-operated dynamo. Apply the electrodes on your neck above the thyroid glands and turn the wheel five times. This is good enough to keep you active even at eighty or ninety.

This will keep you fit and fulfil all the day's hard work without showing any fatigue even though you are in advanced senility.

## Chapter VIII
## HOME TREATMENT OF DISEASES

1. *Abortion:* In cases of abortion let the patient have absolute rest in bed. Avoid strong purgatives and enemas. If there is constipation, give a small quantity of castor oil in coffee. Keep her in bed for a week after all symptoms have subsided.

2. An abortion, however slight, should never be neglected. The broken skin will allow germs to enter the blood. Apply iodex or tincture iodine or boric powder.

3. If the bleeding is slight and the pain trifling, abortion may be prevented by perfect quiet and rest in bed, in a cool room. In threatening abortion, absorbent cotton-wool saturated with cold water or alum lotion should be applied to the external outlet. A dose of chlorodine, 20 drops in an ounce of water, is highly beneficial.

4. *Anaemia:* For anaemia or poverty of blood whether in men or women, there is no food remedy to rival spinach with its high iron content. Lettuce comes next among vegetables; oranges, lemons and pomegranates come foremost among fruits.

5. Butter or ghee in the diet will provide a safeguard against vitamin A deficiency.

6. *Asthma:* Triphala water taken with honey at bed time and honey taken with water 2 or 3 times a day will give best results in Asthma.

7. *Bad Teeth:* Bad teeth are due to improper cleaning. As a result of decayed teeth many diseases, as Pyorrhoea, dyspepsia, pain in the joints, are produced. Clean the teeth thrice daily. Use Danta Rakshak of "Sivananda Ayurvedic Pharmacy": it has proved to be highly beneficial. Clean the teeth with mustard oil and salt. This is a very useful combination.

8. The juice of lemon in a tumblerful of water, either hot or cold, in the early morning, will clean the stomach and intestines,

## HOME TREATMENT OF DISEASES

purify the blood and remove biliousness, skin disease and spongy, bleeding gums.

9. *Brain Tonic:* Soak ten almonds in water at night. Remove the skin in the morning. Take them in the morning with one or two table-spoonfuls of honey. This is a potent brain tonic.

10. *Constipation:* Constipation is one of the commonest ailments. Most persons suffer from this disease and suffer in a variety of ways, too.

11. The causes of constipation are varied. Some people's intestines are weak from birth. Wrong food, wrong habits of eating, also cause constipation. If the intestines do not contain enough waste matter to stimulate it into action, constipation is caused.

12. Where there is a tendency to constipation, the diet should contain a liberal supply of fruits and vegetables. Water should be drunk freely on rising and between meals.

13. Diet is of greater importance in all cases of constipation than any medicine. Drink water freely. Take fruits, figs, plenty of vegetables and fruits.

14. Drink plenty of pure water. The blood will be cleansed of waste and poisonous matter.

15. Live on juicy fruits for a week. This will help greatly towards the elimination of impurities from the system.

16. A simple enema of a teaspoonful of glycerine is highly beneficial.

17. In treatment of constipation, *Hunyadi Janos* water is ideal.

18. A teaspoonful of honey every day will keep the stomach in order for ever.

19. A very large majority of the destructive chronic diseases can be traced to these twin evils—constipation and indigestion. Take Triphala. Do Bhujanga, Salabha, Dhanura and Paschimottanasanas.

20. *Consumption:* Consumption, diabetes, malaria, asthma are costly diseases. They will empty the purse of a man quickly.

21. The successful treatment of consumption lies in pure air, proper rest, good, nourishing food, relief from cares and worries, practice of Bhastrika Pranayama or mild, deep breathing exercises.

22. Diarrhoea or looseness of the bowels may be caused by some irritation. The best remedy is a dose of castor oil. This frees the bowels of any irritant. Do not attempt to stop diarrhoea by opium as is done often.

23. There are various kinds of diarrhoea, viz., diarrhoea premonitory of cholera, diarrhoea premonitory of dysentery, diarrhoea accompanying other diseases, irritative diarrhoea, diarrhoea of atmospheric changes or chill, hill diarrhoea and infantile diarrhoea. Do not check the diarrhoea at once. First remove all irritants by taking a mild purgative, Enos' Fruit Salt or Castor oil or Triphala water.

24. *Dysentery:* In acute cases of dysentery the patient must be confined to bed. The food must be fluid, water, barley-water, milk, etc. Take a dose of castor oil emulsion and then take Bismuth mixture 3 times daily.

25. Buttermilk is very cooling to the system. It quenches thirst. It is useful in diseases of the stomach and intestines. It is useful in dysentery. The lactic acid contained in buttermilk kills the pathogenic germs that may be present in the stomach and bowels.

26. Isafgul and Bael are valuable adjuncts in dysentery. Emetine Bismuth Iodide is a favourite combination.

27. *Dyspepsia:* Dyspeptics should have regular exercise in the open air and give careful attention to the teeth. They should take meals at regular hours and masticate their food well. They should have regular action of the bowels.

28. *Excessive Thirst: Do* not take a large quantity of salt. Avoid too much of pickles and spiced dishes. Eat plenty of fruits. You will not feel too much thirst.

29. *Flatulence:* Flatulence or generation of gas in the stomach and the intestines is one of the commonest symptoms of indigestion. Take powder of ginger along with milk, a dose of

carminative mixture. Practise Paschimottanasana, Agnisara, Uddyana Bandha, regularly. Flatulence will take to its heels.

30. *General:* Do not play with symptoms of disease. It is much more simple to prevent than to cure.

31. Those who tell you that they will cure you of a chronic digestive trouble or any chronic ailment within a couple of days by giving you a drug are either fools or cheats. Believe them not.

32. *Giddiness:* Giddiness or vertigo is a sensation. It is dizziness or swooning not amounting to actual fainting. Objects appear to be moving in different directions. There is a sense of dimness or darkness. There is loss of power to balance the body. There is mental confusion. Perhaps sounds of bells or drums are heard. It is a symptom rather than a disease. It may be due to debility, indigestion, too much of mental work, excess of tobacco or alcohol. Discover the cause and treat it. Take rest and inhale ammonia carb or sal volatile.

33. *Headache:* Headache is not a disease by itself but a symptom of disease, and a very common symptom. Discover the cause and remove it.

34. Eye strain, constipation, insufficient sleep, indigestion, biliousness, breathing stuffy air are all causes for headache. Remove the cause. You will have no headache.

35. *Indigestion:* If you have a feeling of heaviness in the stomach for more than one hour, it means that you have taken heavy food or that there has been a wrong combination.

36. If there is anorexia or distaste for food or indigestion, take Hingu Ashtak Churna or Bhaskar Lavan Churna or Kshudha Vardhak before or after meals.

37. *Leprosy:* If persons suffering from leprosy and other skin diseases strip themselves of all clothing and remain naked in the sun till their body is properly tanned, then the sun rays will penetrate their body and work wonders there.

38. *Malaria:* Malaria kills more people than any other disease. It is the cause of the greatest economic loss. Sleep within mosquito net. Apply citronelle oil to the exposed parts at night. Take 3 grains of quinine as a preventive. Keep the surroundings

of your house clean. Bury all broken parts and tins. Keep the place dry. Use D.D.T. Spray.

39. Mix one drachm of citronella oil with 2 ounces of vaseline and apply this to the exposed parts. This will prevent mosquito and sand-fly bites.

40. Milk-abscess appears on the breast of a nursing mother, on account of lack of cleanliness or of malnutrition. Wean the child at once. Apply hot fomentation to the parts every two or three hours.

41. *Nocturnal Emission:* Spermatorrhoea or wet-dream troubles young boys very much. It is a common disease of the young age, but now it has become more general.

*Causes:* Constipation, dyspepsia, bladder troubles and certain bad habits are at the root of this disease.

Cinema-going, reading of novels, mixing too much with young girls and thoughts about women and sexual matters are also responsible for this common enemy of the youth.

One should not mind if the discharge of semen is occasional. The immediate cause of the emission is thinking about sensual pleasures. Another one is pressure of urine on the bladder and of hard faecal matter on the bowels.

The first precaution to be taken is to abstain from such kind of thoughts. The second one is to see that the evacuation of the faecal matter is natural. The third one is to empty the bladder whenever it is full, and never to stop the urge for urination or the evacuation of the bowels.

In case of constipation, use of enema is most essential. The use of laxative is of not much benefit, as this creates heat in the body. To relieve the pressure on the bladder, little or practically no liquid or solid food should be taken after sunset, and the bladder should be emptied before going to bed.

*Food remedies:* One should live on fruits, at least for a week. During the next week, he should take fruits and milk or buttermilk. After a fortnight he should have his ordinary morning meal, and in the evening he should take fruits and milk only. If possible, he should take hip or sitz bath for ten minutes a day for a month. He should take a morning walk or run a mile or take some kind of exercise or do Surya Namaskar. He should avoid tea, coffee, onions, garlic, cabbage, cauliflower. He should wear a Langoti or Chaddi always. He should avoid lying on the back.

Complete cure may take at least one to six months, according to the intensity of the disease. If the disease is of long-standing, the cure may take a long time, as Nature's processes are slow but sure. Whenever he is haunted by sensual thoughts, he should try to entertain thoughts about his favourite deity.

He may do the following Asanas: (1) Paschimottanasana, (2) Bhujangasana, (3) Vajrasana. He may do each Asana for a minute or two in the beginning. He should sleep on his side, especially left side, and not on the back.

He may take two grains of camphor in two ounces of milk in the evening. He may use Brahmacharya Sudha of "Sivananda Ayurvedic Pharmacy". Lastly, he should have self-confidence. Diseases or difficulties do not last for ever. They are temporary. He should try to fight them with courage and use his will-power to conquer them. If he will help himself, God is sure to help him. God is always kind and just. He sends diseases and distresses to test us. These trials are good for building our character and we must face them with boldness.

42. A cold hip-bath prevents wet-dreams.

43. *Palpitation:* A throbbing or fluttering of heart is felt distinctly. This is palpitation. It is a symptom of many forms of dyspepsia. It may be caused by over-indulgence in tobacco, alcohol, tea or coffee.

44. Palpitation is seldom the sign of any serious disease. Avoid excessive, violent exercises and indigestible food. Tobacco, coffee, tea and alcohol should be given up altogether or taken in strict moderation.

45. Palpitation is a symptom not specially cardiac. It is apt to arouse in the patient's mind the suspicion that he suffers from heart disease. Be not afraid. Be not alarmed unnecessarily. Be bold. Be cheerful. It will pass away quickly. Take rest and a tonic such as Chandraprabha (Sivananda Ayurvedic Pharmacy) or Nux Vomica.

46. *Piles:* The rectum or lower gut is a terminal point in which a number of arteries and veins meet. It is a dependent part. Blood is liable to stagnate here especially if any obstruction occurs, by liver affection or by obstinate constipation. Therefore, piles develop. If there is no constipation, there is no piles. Therefore have a free movement of the bowels somehow or other in the early morning.

47. External piles show bluish bead-like projection. The name for piles is haemorrhoids. The Hindi name is Bhavaseer.

48. Piles is always due to constipation. Keep the bowels free. You will have no piles. Nip the malady in the bud. Take plenty of vegetables and fruits. Do Sarvangasana and Maha Mudra.

49. *Renal Colic:* During renal colic place the patient in a hot bath. Foment the loins. Give barley water in abundance.

50. A tepid hip-bath stops renal colic and helps the free flow of menstrual fluid and urine.

51. *Uvula:* Uvula is a fleshy body that hangs down at the back of the mouth. It is liable to increase in length owing to cold and will cause irritation and cough. Touch it with Tannic acid, glycerine or mandal's pigment. Use alum gargle. Put a few grains of salt in warm water and gargle the throat.

52. *Wart:* If there are warts, apply a strong solution of acetic acid. Touch the wart lightly with the acid. Do not allow the acid to fall on the surrounding skin.

53. *Water Remedies:* Water is a component of our body, and so it can cure many diseases. I shall, therefore, deal with cold and hot water cures.

*The uses of cold water:* For any kind of pain which is not acute, use a cold pack covered with a woollen cloth. In slight disorders of the eyes, you can wash your eyes frequently with cold water. For toothache of a mild nature, take a mouthful of cold water, keep it in the mouth till it becomes a little warm and blow it out after a few seconds. Do this four or five times. To avoid cold and catarrah, take a small basin of water, fill it to the brim, close one nostril with your fingers of one hand and, taking the basin of water in the other hand, suck the water through the nostril which is open. Now close the other nostril and suck water through the first nostril. Do this three or four times a day in the morning.

In case of cold and catarrah, apply a wet cold pack round the neck at bed time. Keep it covered with woollen cloth. For headache keep a cold water pack over your forehead or on the head for a few minutes. Cold pack over the abdomen cures many diseases of the urinary system, bladder and of the bowels. For slight burns, bruises and cuts, apply cold bandage to that part. For easy bowel action, drink a tumblerful of drinking water as soon as you get up. Cold hip-bath or sitz bath taken daily for ten to fifteen minutes cures many chronic diseases.

*Uses of hot water:* Hot-water drinking, at least half an hour before meals, daily, for some days, cures constipation. For acute pains and swelling, use hot fomentations or hot water pack. Putting your feet dipped in hot water which is bearable for ten minutes cures cold and gives sound sleep.

## Chapter IX
## SPIRITUAL ROAD TO HEALTH AND HAPPINESS
### TEN COMMANDMENTS
1. Practise Truthfulness, Non-violence and Celibacy.
2. Be good, do good.
3. Be tolerant.
4. Be kind to all.
5. Serve all; serve the Lord in all; love all.
6. Share with others what you have.
7. Think rightly; act rightly.
8. Give, purify, meditate, realise.
9. Behold the One Self in all. See God in every face.
10. Feel "I am the all-pervading Immortal Self".

### TWENTY-SIX PRECEPTS

1. Yoga brings a message of hope to the forlorn, joy to the depressed, strength to the weak and knowledge to the ignorant.

2. Fear is the deadliest disease. It is the cause of worldly cares and anxieties. Remove this by cultivating courage and meditation on the fearless Atman or Immortal Self.

3. Temperance, exercise, pure air, wholesome food, rest, refreshing sleep, God's Name, are the best of all physicians.

4. Mere wholesome diet, fresh air, exercise, alone cannot give you lasting health and happiness. Spiritual life alone can bestow real health and happiness.

5. The mind vibrates discordantly, the five sheaths vibrate inharmoniously, on account of the force of Rajas (passion) and Tamas (inertia), likes and dislikes, lust, greed, hatred, fear and jealousy. How can you expect real happiness and health when such a state of affairs prevails in the system.

6. Mental health is more vital than bodily health. diseases take their origin in the mind first, and then manifest in the physical body (Adhi-Vyadhi).

7. Do not think of a disease too much. Too much thinking of the disease intensifies and strengthens the disease. Forget the body and the disease. Keep the mind fully occupied on useful works.

8. Abandon imaginary fears, unnecessary worries, cares and anxieties. Have perfect faith in God and do the right.

9. When you are small boys, you have tummy aches and bilious attacks. When you are young, you get egoistic-fever, lust-fever, anger-fever, jealousy-fever. When you become old, you get headaches. Remove Tamas (inertia), Moha (lust), Mahamoha, Tamas (inertia) born of egoism, Raga and Dvesha. Get knowledge of Self and attain eternal health and happiness.

10. The practice of Pranayama has a wonderful influence over the body, the mind, the intellect and the senses.

11. Pranayama regulates the breath and the mind also. There are harmonious vibrations. You will enjoy good health and happiness. Therefore be regular in your daily practice of Pranayama.

12. The practice of 'Asanas' develops the body, and the practitioner is agile and nimble. He has a very elastic spine and a supple body.

13. Practise Brahmacharya. Entertain pure, divine thoughts. Study sacred books. Have Satsanga. Dwell in the company of saints.

14. He who boasts "I have never had any disease in this life" has lost the greatest lesson of life, the most beautiful lecture in that great school of humanity, the sick chamber.

15. Disease is, indeed, a blessing. It opens your eyes to the realities of life. It instils mercy and sympathy in your heart and turns your mind towards God.

16. When a man is suffering from an acute, unbearable pain, he abandons his vanity and recollects that there is God. He becomes humble and penitent.

17. If you visit a patient, do not talk about his diseases, cheer him up. Talk on spiritual matters. Tell him some stories of saints or great Mahatmas and their great deeds. Make him laugh

through educative humour. Do Kirtan and Mrityunjaya Japa with him. This is a potent, an unfailing tonic.

18. Cultivate divine virtues, such as purity, magnanimity, humility, cosmic love, courage, forgiveness. Then there will be harmony and peace in the mind, and consequently you will enjoy real, good health and happiness.

19. Enquire 'who am I?' There cannot be any disease in the ever pure, all-pervading, immortal, diseaseless soul. Disease belongs to the material body and not to the resplendent Spirit or Soul.

20. The ingredients of health and long life are prayer, Japa, Kirtan, meditation, serenity, cosmic love, temperance, regulated life, fresh open air, regular exercise, regulated breathing exercises or Pranayama, sun-bath and good wholesome food.

21. Do unconditional and unreserved self-surrender to the Lord. He will take care of you. Be at ease. You will be free from fear and worries. You will enjoy health and happiness.

22. Practise the presence of God. Behold Him in all faces, in all beings, in all forms. See Him everywhere. You will enjoy real peace, health and happiness.

23. Prayer, Kirtan, Japa and meditation fill the mind with Sattva. Divine energy flows from the Lord to the devotee. He enjoys real lasting health and happiness.

24. Meditate ceaselessly on the desireless, ever blissful Atman. Chant OM. Sing OM. Do Japa of OM. You will be blessed with health and happiness.

## HEALING THE SICK

Meditation can work wonders in healing the sick. Meditation by sick persons themselves is very effective. It is possible for a third person to do it for the sufferer. The method is thus:—Chant OM OM OM. If you have a secluded place, do a few rounds of Bhastrika and a few rounds of Sukha-Purvak Pranayama. Feel, as you inhale, that the Lord's Healing Power is flowing into you, and at Kumbhaka, as if it is filling your entire being. Soham Japa for a little while will help you to raise your own consciousness to a high level.

Then sit by the bed-side of the patient. Remain calm, serene and meditative. It is better not to let the mind be disturbed by any thought, especially of the disease. Now, with open eyes, concentrate on the heart of the sick person. Feel, feel and feel intensely the Presence of the Anamaya (diseaseless) Atman there. Feel that the Atman which is in you is in him too. Connect the two: merge one in the other: meditate now deeply. After this Process is over, feel for a few minutes that the Lord's Healing Power has filled the patient and that he is better. Now, cheer him up with consoling words. You will find the patient yielding rapidly to this treatment. After the treatment is over, go again into meditation and recharge yourself with His Healing Power.

## YOGA FOR HEALTH

Most of the diseases take their origin in over-eating, sexual excess and outbursts of anger and hatred. If the mind is kept cool and calm at all times, you will have wonderful health, strength and vitality. Energy is depleted by fits of anger. The cells and tissues are filled with morbid, poisonous materials, when one loses his temper and entertains deep hatred. Various sorts of physical ailments crop up. The blood becomes hot and thin and consequently night-pollutions result. Various kinds of nervous diseases are attributable to excessive loss of the seminal energy and frequent fits of explosive anger or wrath.

Let any disease remain in your body. Do not bother much. Do not fret and fume. Develop the powers of endurance and resistance. Strengthen your body, mind and nerves. Take plenty of open-air exercises, substantial nutritious food, medicated oil bath and plenty of rest. Have mental and physical recreation. Lead a well-regulated life. Be moderate in food, drink and enjoyments. Lead a spiritual life. All diseases will leave your body by themselves. All microbes will die, when your vitality, vigour and strength are at a flood-tide. This is the secret of health and happiness.

Do not be carried away by the pompous advertisements made by quacks and charlatans. Lead a simple natural life. You will become all right soon. Do not spend any money in purchasing the so-called patent medicines and specifics. They are worthless.

Quacks try to exploit the credulous and the ignorant. Beware. Do not go to the doctors very often. Endeavour to qualify yourself as your own doctor. Understand the laws of nature and the principles of hygiene and health. Do not trespass against the laws of health.

Bask in the Sun. Expose your body to the rays of the Sun for a short time daily. This is heliotherapy or Sun-treatment. The Sun is the source of energy and power. You will derive energy and power from the Sun.

Soak 12 almonds at night. Remove the skin and take the almonds with some sugarcandy in the early morning. Or you can make a refreshing beverage by grinding these almonds with a little black pepper and sugarcandy. This is called "thandai" by the Punjabis. This is a fine, cooling and strength-giving tonic.

Rest in bed is necessary. Adjust your diet. Take simple, wholesome, easily digestible, bland and non-irritating food. Give up hot, pungent curries, chutneys and chillies. Rest the stomach and the small bowels by taking recourse to partial fasts. If you can fast for whole day, it is all the better. Fasting eliminates poisons and overhauls the system thoroughly. You can take sago and milk, barley water and fruits like sweet oranges, grapes, etc. If you are thirsty, you can take lemon-juice with sugarcandy.

Observe Brahmacharya. Get up at 4 a.m. and practise Japa of *"Hari Om"* or any Mantra and also meditation for one hour. The Name of the Lord is the best medicine or tonic in the world. You should have intense faith in the power of the Names of the Lord. Incurable diseases are cured by Japa or singing Hari's Name. Meditation creates new, healthy vibrations in all the cells of the body and removes any kind of disease. All the tissues are bathed in the nectar that flows during meditation. All disease-causing germs are destroyed. The rationale of this kind of Yogic or spiritual treatment is yet unknown to the medical profession.

Why do you unnecessarily introduce foreign drugs into the system? Resort to Nature-cure and Yogic-Chikitsa. Practise regularly Pranayama, breathing exercises, Asanas, concentration and meditation. This is the ideal treatment. Do not think too much of the disease and too much of the body. Too much thinking of the disease will intensify the malady. Keep the mind fully occupied in some way or the other, this is very important. Take away the mind from the body and think of the diseaseless Atman or Soul within, the bed-rock or substratum for the body mind. Friend, cultivate this kind of Atma-chintan and attain the *Anamaya-pada* or Painless Seat—Param Dhama or Immortal Brahman. Cheer yourself up, brother. Have a cheerful countenance always. Meditate on OM. Think of OM. Sing OM. OM is thy real name. OM is the best tonic, specific or sheet-anchor, panacea or cure-all, "pick me up" or sovereign remedy for all diseases. Smile and laugh. Thou art bodiless, the undying Soul. Never, never forget this.

May God bless you with perfect health, high standard of vigour, strength, vitality and longevity. May you prosper gloriously.

## VEDANTA FOR HEALTH

The Atman or the Self that resides in the chambers of your heart is the storehouse for health, strength, vigour and vitality. It cannot be affected by germs, microbes, bacilli and cocci. Cholera, pyorrhoea, plague, etc., cannot touch it. Weakness, depression, uneasiness, feeling out of sorts and morbidity, have no place there. Germs and a host of diseases take to their heels, if any one simply remembers the Atman or one's own Self.

The best medicine or tonic for any complaint, physical or mental (Adhi and Vyadhi), is constant thinking: "I am the Spirit or Atman which is independent of the body and mind and which is Anamaya (diseaseless)." Even if you think this once, it will give immense inner strength and elevation. If a habit of thinking in this direction is formed definitely, it is a solace, comfort and mental peace. This is the cheap, potent, easily available medicine that lies at your command, that is very close to you, that is within easy access or approach. Practise this. Feel this. Be assured of the efficacy of this divine tonic. You can save much money, time and energy. The vast majority do not avail themselves of this rare panacea, though they have very often heard of this from saints and spiritual books and Srutis. This is due to deep ignorance and lack of faith. People are immersed in worldliness. They are engrossed in passion and Samsaric activities. They have no time to think of this inner, real, unfailing, remedy. They have neither leisure for nor interest in doing introspection and self-analysis. The world is now flooded with multifarious injections such as insulin, vitamin, neosalvarsan, etc., and patents of beverages and tonics. People are carried away by pompous advertisements. Money is wasted enormously in paying doctors' bills. They immediately run to find relief in outside objects and from physical doctors, who despite their qualifications and degrees, are still ignorant of many things, who are still groping in darkness, who are yet not able to diagnose when there is a complication, who have no real genuine specifics to cure diseases like asthma, malaria, lumbago, phthisis, cerebro-spinal-meningitis, typhoid, diabetes, blood-pressure, etc., who are still only experimenting on the patients, who are greedy, who do not take real interest in the patients, who have neither sympathy nor Atma Bhav, who have no knowledge of the proper suggestions. Even when there is no trace of phthisis, by their saying: "Oh! You have got T.B. You must go to the Sanatorium at Bhowali or Alps." The poor patient actually develops phthisis on account of fear caused by the destructive suggestion of the ignorant doctor. Sympathetic doctors are very rare. How can you expect real solace and comfort from a doctor who has neither sympathy nor mercy, who has no Training in Nishkamya Karma Yoga and who is intent on accumulating wealth?

A noble doctor is one who says with sympathy and mercy even when a patient is in a dying condition: "Friend, don't be afraid. This disease is nothing. You will be all right in no time. This medicine will give you strength and vitality and make you quite fit." Mere kind encouraging words from the mouth of a doctor or anybody are a great blessing. They infuse new strength, new vigour and new vitality into the distressed patient. The patient is pulled round by the strength of these sweet words even without medicine.

A doctor may object: "Swamiji, I cannot get any practice if I say like this. I cannot maintain myself. I will have to close my dispensary if I subscribe to this." My answer is: "If the doctor behaves in the above manner and if he follows my instructions, he will have a roaring practice. He will be the foremost and best doctor in the city. People will flock in thousands to a kind, sympathetic doctor. They will place their very lives at his feet and sacrifice everything unto him. He will get the blessings of the patients and the fruits of their good Sankalpas. He will amass enormous wealth. They will pay him amply, willingly, with pure feeling of love from the bottom of their hearts." Oh, doctors! Practise this method and see whether you get money or not.

That doctor who has no knowledge of the "Science of Suggestions" cannot do much good to the people. That doctor who gives a destructive, negative suggestion to the patient does immense harm and fatal injury. The doctor who has neither sympathy nor patience, who has no Atma Bhav, who fails to see the Self in all living beings, who simply uses his knowledge for accumulating wealth, lives in vain. His lot is pitiable, indeed! He has eyes but sees not. Will a doctor dare charge heavy bills, if once he has clearly understood that the same Atman which dwells in his own heart resides in all these patients?

In olden days, an ordinary Vaidya (doctor) would cure a disease with some bazaar drugs worth about two pies. In these days of modern civilisation and scientific advancement, allopathic medical treatment has become very costly. Poor people cannot afford to have this. The Patient has to get examined his blood, urine, faeces and sputum. He has to visit the Sapta-Rishis of medical profession. He has to go to a bacteriologist first for this purpose and has to jingle something at the table. The bacteriologist directs the patient to go to a dentist to remove the tartar and treat his pyorrhoea, which is believed to be the root cause of all diseases. He has to pay him Rs. 10/-. Then he has to go to the radiologist for taking a skyagraph in the X-rays. He has to pay him Rs. 25/-. Sometimes he has to pay the board of doctors for expert diagnosis. He finds no real relief even after spending much money.

Repeat the following formulae mentally several times daily. Meditate on the meaning. Chronic, incurable diseases that are declared hopeless by a board of eminent doctors can be cured by this method. This is an unfailing, infallible, divine remedy.

Sometimes you will have to wait patiently for results. Auto-suggestion is only an offshoot of Vedanta. The formulae of this school, viz.,

"Through the grace of God, I am becoming better and better, day by day, in every way" is only a Vedantic assertion and affirmation.

Sing now, feel and assert

| | | |
|---|---|---|
| 1. | Ananda Svarupoham | Om Om Om |
| | I am an embodiment of happiness | Om Om Om |
| | I am Bliss in Essence | Om Om Om |
| 2. | Anamayoham | Om Om Om |
| | I am diseaseless Atman | Om Om Om |
| 3. | I am all-health | Om Om Om |
| 4. | I am neither body nor mind | Om Om Om |
| 5. | I am the embodiment of Arogyam | Om Om Om |
| 6. | No disease or germ can enter my body | Om Om Om |
| 7. | My will is pure and irresistible | Om Om Om |

People say: "One apple a day keeps the doctor away."

This is costly. This is doubtful. I say: "Live in the spirit of the above formulae. This alone can keep the doctor away. This is dead cheap. This is a sure sovereign specific and a sheet-anchor and a cure-all. Doctors' bills and money can be saved. This will give you Self-realisation as well." Believe me; give up doubting. I assure you, my dear brother! Thou art not this perishable body. Thou art the immortal, all-pervading soul. "Tat Tvam Asi—Thou art that." Rejoice in Sat-Chit-Ananda Atman within and become a Jivanmukta in this very birth.

May you all free yourselves from disease, death and birth!

## KARMA

Man gets good health on account of good Karma done in his previous birth. He who had done meritorious services in his previous incarnation, he who had shared what he had with others, he who had helped the poor and the needy, he who had done worship, meditation, Yogic Kriyas and Pranayama in his previous births, enjoys sound health in this birth. The law of causation is inexorable and unrelenting.

## ATMA JNANA

What is the highest thing that a man can achieve in this world? It is Self-realisation. What are the advantages or benefits of this Self-realisation? Why should we attempt at Self-realisation at all? The attainment of Atma Jnana or realisation of the identity of Jiva and Brahman can alone put an end to the wheel of birth and death and its concomitant evils of disease, old age, pain, sufferings, miseries, worries and various sorts of trouble. It is Atma Jnana alone that can give unalloyed, eternal bliss, supreme peace, highest knowledge and immortality.

## HEALTH AND MIND

You must be free from Adhi and Vyadhi (diseases of the mind and the body), if you want to attain peace of mind and knowledge of the Self. According to the Science of Yoga, all physical diseases take their origin in the disease of the mind, from an unhealthy state of mind. Western psychologists also corroborate the fact. They say that the diseases of the body are attributable to hatred, anger, worry, depression etc., which corrode the mind and react on the body and bring about various sorts of physical diseases by destroying the cells of the body.

You should have an elementary knowledge of Raja Yoga, psychology, Ayurveda, physiology, family medicine, hygiene, Sankhya and Vedanta philosophy. Then you will be able to keep up your health nicely. You must have a knowledge of the laws, the nature, habits and ways of the mind. Then only can you keep up a clean and healthy mind always. No one can work smoothly with a ruffled mind. A ruffled mind disturbs the three humours of the body and brings about all sorts of diseases in its turn. This is the theory of Ayurveda which quite tallies with the theory of Western psychologists and the theory of Raja Yoga.

At every second various kinds of vibrations from the various kinds of objects of the physical universe outside enter the mind of a man and produce various kinds of influence. Body is part of the universe. So is the mind. What is called the world is the mind only—*Mano-Matram Jagat, Manah Kalpitam Jagat.* The mind of a man is affected by the thoughts and opinions of others. There is pressure of thought from outside. You must have immense strength to act against these outside thoughts. Have courage, patience and perseverance. With asinine patience, adamantine will and determination and with leech-like tenacity, you will get success in all your attempts.

## SANKHYA PHILOSOPHY

Study of Sankhya philosophy will give you a knowledge of the law of the universe, and the operation of the world, creation of the universe, how the mind is formed, how the organs of action and sensation are formed, what are the Tanmatras or rudimentary root elements, what is Mahat Tattva, what is Purusha and Prakriti, what are the three Gunas, how they operate and influence a man, how they affect the health and mentality of a man, and how to get knowledge of Purusha. Sankhya and the Yoga of Patanjali Maharshi are complementary. Vedanta is only an amplification and fulfilment of Sankhya.

## HEALTH AND ASTROLOGY

An elementary knowledge of astrology is of immense use. The movement of the earth round the sun brings about the various Ritus or seasons. The atmospheric conditions affect the body, The various seasons have a distinct bearing on the health of man. The planets have a direct influence of the mind and body of man. They exercise benign or malevolent influence on man in accordance with their position in the various houses. He who has some knowledge of astrology can ward off the evil effects of unfavourable planets.

May all enjoy Perfect Health, strength and Long Life!

"*Lokah Samasthah Sukhino Bhavantu*".

## VEDANTIC COMPRESSED TABLET

There is the Saccharin tablet
For the diabetic patients.
There is the Amyal Nitras tablet
For the patients of Angina Pectoris.
There is the Ephadrein tablet
For the Asthmatics;

You have all sorts of tablets,
For all sorts of diseases.
This is the age of tablets—
Park Davis and Burroughs-Welcome
Are day in and day out
Manufacturing tablets,
Yet the diseases are not cured;
New diseases are cropping up,
New 'ities', new 'orrheas'.
Sivananda says:
Use these Vedantic compressed tablets
Of Upanishadic essence;
They are the four Mahavakyas—
*Prajnanam Brahma, Aham Brahma Asmi,
Tat Tvam Asi, Ayam Atma Brahma.*
Each Mahavakya contains
The essence of one Veda.
The whole world is compressed in OM.
All diseases will be cured,
Feel: *Anamayoham*—I am the diseaseless Atman.

## VEDANTIC VITAMIN

This is an age of vitamin;—
The market abounds with
Vitamin A, B, C, D, E, F, G.
Allopaths do not use mixtures now.
They at once inject with Vitamin A, etc.,
For any kind of disease.
This itself is a disease of the doctors.
They must be injected first with
The potent Vedantic Vitamin.
This Vedantic Vitamin is a cure-all.
It cures the disease of birth and death.
It cures the disease of ignorance.
It removes fear, lust, greed,
It generates knowledge:
This Vitàmin is Pranava or OM!
Sivananda says:

O Ram! Take this Vitamin of vitamins.
That is prepared in the laboratory of sages.
And do not take any more body,
Ask for "Brahman's Brand" only.
This "Vedantic Vitamin" is Brahman Itself,
The inexhaustible Source for all powers.

## VEDANTIC BEVERAGE

Clean your heart mortar first,
With the water of celibacy.
Put some almonds of faith;
Rub them with the pestle of courage;
Add some black pepper of patience;
And some Brahmi leaves of reflection;
Some cooling seeds of vigilance;
The rose petals of divine grace;
Big cardamoms of introspection;
The colouring substance of tenacity;
Now add the sugar of meditation;
Finally add the water of Immortality.

Sivananda says:
Drink this immortal elixir, O Ram!
Madalasa gave this beverage to her children.
Sulabha drank this joyfully.
This was the favourite drink of Sadasiva Brahman.
Mansoor had this drink always in his heart thermos.

## VEDANTIC TONIC

| | |
|---|---|
| Discrimination | grains 20 |
| Dispassion | grains 40 |
| Serenity | drachm 1 |
| Self-restraint | drachm 2 |
| Endurance | drachm 4 |
| Faith | scruple 1 |
| Renunciation | minims 30 |
| Meditation | drachm 1 |
| Mumukshutva | ounce 1 |

Mix well.

Shake the bottle before use.
Take one ounce twice daily.

Sivananda says:
This tonic will make you bodiless,
It will bestow immortality;
Fast on Ekadasi,
Take saltless diet on Sundays.
Observe Brahmacharya,
Give up onion, garlic,
Cauliflower and turnips,
Meat, liquor and smoking.

## FATTENING AND THINNING OF 3 BODIES

The gross body gets fattened on account of food.
It gets reduced on account of starvation.
The subtle body gets fattened on account of
Raga, Dvesha, desires and egoism.
It gets thinned out on account of
Vairagya, reduction of egoism and desires.
The Causal body gets fattened by Jiva Bhavana.
It gets thinned out by Brahma Bhavana.

## HAVAN FOR CURING TUBERCULOSIS

A Havan has both material as well as spiritual significance. It has got direct action both upon the body as well as the mind of man. The rules laid down in the Varnashrama-Dharma and the daily routine of man as expounded by Manu and others hold good both hygienically and spiritually. They promote the health of the body and evolution of the soul higher up in the path to Spiritual Perfection. A person who strictly follows the rules established by the law of Dharma enjoys good health and long life in this world and attains undecaying bliss afterwards. Daily Havan is one of the compulsory rites prescribed to the Hindu Brahmachari and the householder as well as to the Vanaprastha. The Brahmachari does Samidadhana, the Grihastha keeps Agnihotra and the Vanaprastha continues the same in the forest. Oblations to fire, thus, have got a very important place in the life of man, according to Hindu law.

None, except a Sannyasin, can omit performing daily Havan. This is a part of the eternal Sanatana Dharma. Modern people do not find any sense in daily Ahutis to fire. They think it is mere wastage of food-materials. This is a wrong conception. The greater you give, the more you get. This is the universal law. None can gain except by giving. "Give, and it shall be given to you". Offering to divine beings is more effective than offering to mortal man. It has got immediate effect. With whatever motive the Havan is done, that motive of the person is fulfilled.

Moreover, the materials offered in Havan are great disinfectants. They purify the body, and purify the lungs with the smoke that is inhaled with every breath. There are cases where patients were cured of their long ailments. Tuberculosis is one of the malignant diseases cured by such Havans. Here is given in brief the method of performing the daily Havan.

## MATERIALS NECESSARY FOR HAVAN

Charu is the material which is offered to the fire. It is a mixture of Jav (Yav), Sesamum (Til), rice, ghee, incense (Dhoop) and sandal (Chandan). This is a wonderful combination which will disinfect the whole atmosphere. It is a blessed smoke that is produced from the Yajna-Kunda. The Yajna-Kunda and Ritviks are all purified.

Other materials necessary are camphor, mango leaves, ghee, milk, honey, sugar, curd, Kumkum, turmeric powder, Yajnopavita, cocoanut, areca nut, betel leaves, rice-powder, and Darbha grass.

## METHOD OF PERFORMING HAVAN

The performer of the Havan should take bath and finish his daily Japa or Sandhya. Then he should draw on the floor a square Mandala with rice or wheat powder. In the middle of the Mandala, the word OM must be written in Sanskrit or in one's own mother-tongue. The Mantra of the Devata to whom oblations are offered should be written inside the Mandala thus drawn. On the right side of the Mandala a Kalasa should be kept. Kalasa means a pot of water filled with mango leaves and with cocoanut and a Kurcha of Darbha over that. The Ishta-Devata

# HAVAN FOR CURING TUBERCULOSIS

should be invoked in this Kalasa through the Ishta-Mantra and Puja to the Ishta-Devata.

In the beginning a prayer must be offered to the Devata to whom the Havan is offered. The turmeric powder is spread over the Mandala. Panchamrita should be prepared with milk, honey, ghee, sugar and curd. Plantain also may be added to the Panchamrita. Akshatas should be prepared with rice and Kumkum mixed together with a little water. This is used to worship the Deity. Yajnopavita should be offered to the Lord. Areca nut and betel leaves are meant for offering to the Deity invoked in the Kalasa.

A little Pranayama and Japa should form the beginning of the Karma. Where other Vedic Mantras are found inconvenient for recitation, the Ishta-Mantra and prayers connected with it may be made use of for offering oblations. Ganesa Puja must be done in the beginning.

In the beginning, one Mala of Ghee-Ahutis with Ishta-Mantra may be offered. Then Charu should be offered with the following Mantras:

Om Pranaya Svaha, Om Apanaya Svaha,
Om Vyanaya Svaha,
Om Udanaya Svaha, Om Samanaya Svaha,
Om Paramatmane Svaha.
Om Bhuh Svaha, Om Bhuvah Svaha,
Om Svah Svaha, Om Bhur-Bhuvah-Svah Svaha.
Om Prithivyai Svaha, Om Adbhayah Svaha,
Om Agnaye Svaha, Om Antarikshya Svaha,
Om Brahmane Svaha, Om Vishnave Svaha,
Om Rudraya Svaha, Om Suryaya Svaha.

Those who know the Vedic Mantras can offer oblations to the nine Grahas (Nava-Grahas) with their Mantras. Others can merely repeat their names and offer Ahutis:

Om Agnaye Svaha, Om Visvadevebhyah Svaha,
Om Prajapataye Svaha, Om Brahmane Svaha.

Those who know the Purusha-Sukta may offer oblations with its sixteen Mantras. This is a powerful Mantra.

In the end one Mala of Ishta-Mantra may be done with offering of Ahutis of Charu. Afterwards a cocoanut filled with a little ghee should be offered as Purna-Ahuti. Even plantains may be offered instead of or in addition to the cocoanut.

Then the performer should perform an Arati with camphor. This has got a very powerful effect upon the system of man.

Prayers should be offered in the end and the Havan-Prasad should be taken.

There is no doubt that the Havan thus done daily will purify the person both physically and mentally. This should form part of the daily routine of man.

## DIVINE NAMAPATHY

When allopathy, homoeopathy, chromopathy, naturopathy, Ayurvedapathy and all other 'pathies' fail to cure a disease, the Divine Namapathy alone can save you. The name of the Lord is a sovereign specific, a sheet-anchor, an infallible panacea and a cure-all for all diseases. It is an ideal or supreme "pick me up" in gloom and despair, in depression and sorrow, in the daily battle of life or the struggle for existence. There is a mysterious power in the Name! There is an inscrutable Sakti in God's name! All the divine potencies are hidden in the Lord's name. It is a cream or the quintessence of Chyavan Prash, Makaradhvaja, almonds, Vasanta-Kusumakara or Svarna Bhasma or gold oxide. It is a mysterious, ineffable, divine injection "1910194".

You can take this medicine of Nama Japa yourself for curing any disease. You can administer this marvellous medicine to other patients also in your house or elsewhere. Sit by the side of the patient and repeat the Name of the Lord with sincere devotion and faith like Hari Om, Sri Ram, Om Namah Sivaya and sing His Names also *"Hare Rama Hare Rama Rama Rama Hare Hare, Hare Krishna Hare Krishna Krishna Krishna Hare Hare"*. Pray for His Mercy and grace. All maladies and agonies will come to an end. Do the treatment of Nama Japa for at least two hours in the morning and evening. You will find the miraculous effect within a short time. Both the doctor and the patient should have perfect faith in the Lord's Name. His mercy and grace. The real doctor is only Lord Narayana. Lord Dhanvantari, the physician of the three worlds (who expounded the Ayurvedic Medical Science), has himself declared "By the medicine of the repetition of Achyuta, Ananta, Govinda, all diseases are cured.... this is my definite and honest declaration." In all treatments Lord Narayana is the real doctor. You find that even the world's best doctors fail to cure a dying king. You might have also heard of many instances where patients ailing from the worst type of diseases are cured miraculously where even the ablest doctors have declared the case hopeless. This itself is clear proof that there is the Divine Hand behind all cures.

The Divine Name will eradicate the disease of birth and death and bestow on you Moksha, liberation or Immortality.

The son of a landlord in Meerut was seriously ailing. Doctors pronounced the case to be absolutely hopeless. Bhaktas took the case in their hands. They did continuous Kirtan day and night for seven days around the bed of the patient. The patient stood up and began to sing God's Name on the seventh day. He recovered completely. Such is the miraculous power of Sankirtan.

## MOKSHA RASAYANA

Here is a cheap, patent specific for obtaining Moksha (Bliss). Prepare the medicine as prescribed in the following page and stir it in the vessel of your brain for 24 hours. Heat it in the fire of Vairagya and cleanse it with Viveka. Sweeten it with the syrup of Mumukshutva and the elixir of meditation (on *Om* or *Tat Tvam Asi* Mahavakya). Put it in the bottle of your heart and cork the bottle with Sraddha and Samadhana. Drink one teaspoonful every two hours as prescribed. This is a Sovereign Remedy for the dire disease of birth and death, prepared in the Brahma-Jnana Research Pharmacy of Siva at "Ananda Kutir", Rishikesh (Himalayas). This specific can be had from all Ashrams, Mutts, Sannyasis, Yogis, Jnanis and all Sadhus. It is priced to suit everybody's pocket: (Inland) Suddha Prem and full Sraddha; (Foreign) simple living and high thinking.

## AN ADHYATMIC PRESCRIPTION
### "TAT TVAM ASI"

Tele { Grams: "Para Brahman"  Consulting Hours:
Phone: 1.  AT ALL TIMES

**BRAHMA-JNANA RESEARCH PHARMACY**
**"ANAND KUTIR"**
**RISHIKESH** (Himalayas).

Consulting Doctor: Dr. BRAHMAN.
J.M. (Niralambapuri)  (Jivanmukta)

CODES:

Prasthana Traya.        B.N. (Brahmanishtha)
Brahma Sutras.          (Brahmapuri)
Ten Upanishads.         B.L. (Brahmaleen)
Gita.                   (Mt. Kailas)

Specialist in Brahma-Vidya.

Brahman's Patent: Brahma Rasayana (EXTRA STRONG).
Prescription No. 0000000000.
Name: Brahman Om.
Sex: Sexless Atman.
Disease: Birth and death.
Caste: Self.
Age: Eternity.
X-Ray findings: Moola Ajnana in Karanasarira and Vasanas in the mind.
Diet: Sattvic food.

### RECIPE (Take Thou)

| | | |
|---|---|---|
| Commonsense | ... ... | gr. 1 |
| Prudence | ... ... | gr. ½ |
| Self-reliance | ... ... | gr. ½ |
| Faith | ... ... | drachm 1 |
| Understanding | ... ... | drachm 1 |
| Patience | ... ... | oz 1 |
| Perseverance. | ... ... | oz 6 |
| Resolution | ... ... | lb 1 |
| Vairagya | ... ... | oz 8 |

# AN ADHYATMIC PRESCRIPTION

| Viveka | ... ... | q.s. (quantity sufficient) |
|---|---|---|
| Iron will | ... ... | oz 8 |
| Tranquillity | ... ... | dr 1 |
| Abstraction | ... ... | dr 1 |
| Endurance | ... ... | dr 2 |
| Equanimity | ... ... | dr 4 |
| Syrup Mumukshutva | ... ... | oz 8 |
| Elixir Meditation | ... ... | oz 8 |

Mix

Fiat mixtura (Moksha Rasayana)
Sig:—One teaspoonful every two hours.
PRICE—*Inland:* Suddha Prem and full faith.
*Foreign:* Simple living and high thinking.

(Sd.) *Dr. Brahman.*

## Chapter X

### SEE GOOD IN EVERYTHING

**I**

Brahman or the Eternal is infinite. His expressions also are infinite. Allopathy, Homoeopathy, Hydropathy, Chromopathy, Electropathy, Naturopathy, Ayurveda, Unani are all His expressions. All these systems are very essential. Temperaments are different, natures are different. Therefore different systems of treatment to suit men of different temperaments are also necessary. Only the prejudiced and intolerant man says: "Allopathy is useless. Homoeopathy is the best system. Nature Cure is better. Ayurveda is bad. Unani is good". For some, Ayurvedic medicines are suitable. For some others, Unani medicines do good. For some, Nature Cure is quite suitable. Sun's rays, water, herbs, green leaves, steam, mud plaster are all medicines. They are all products of Prakriti. Only names differ. The very fact that different systems of medicine exist now shows that there is something good in each system.

A busy man of the world or a weak man will find it difficult to fast for days and weeks and months. It will be irksome for him to undergo the treatment prescribed by a Naturopath for months and years. He wants immediate relief and repair. This he finds in Allopathy or Homoeopathy.

Too much drugging is bad. It is always better to avail oneself of Nature's aids. But if a drug can bring back the life of a man when it is trembling in the balance, there is no harm in taking it.

Even molecules, atoms and corpuscles have their loves and hates, their likes and dislikes, attractions and repulsions, affinities and non-affinities. The Allopath, Homoeopath and Naturopath have their own likes and dislikes. Everybody has his own whim and eccentricity to some extent. A naturopath condemns and hates an Allopath. An Allopath dislikes a Naturopath and Naturopathy. A large-hearted doctor, with equal

## SEE GOOD IN EVERYTHING

vision and tolerance and with practical knowledge of Vedanta can appreciate the beauty of variety in Divine expression, can behold the unity in diversity and utilise every system to the best advantage according to time and need.

Some Christians say that one can attain God-realisation only through Christianity and reading the Bible. Some Muslims say that one can attain God-head only by reading the Koran. Some Hindus say that one can reach the goal only if one knows Sanskrit and reads Vyakarana and logic. Even so, a Naturopath says that one can attain health through Naturopathy alone. An Ayurvedic Vaidya declares that one can be healthy only if one follows the Ayurvedic system. Bigotry, fanaticism and eccentricity reign supreme in medical systems also.

An anaemic, weak, patient who has been suffering from poverty of blood for several years can recoup his health in a very short time by taking a course of iron tonic, whereas in Naturopathy he will have to wait for a long time to get his needed iron from the articles of diet.

Every system has its own advantages and bright side. All systems have come from the same one Divine source. Do not fight with one another in proving the superiority of your own system. Take the good in everything. Be tolerant. Become wise and happy. Lead a healthy life. Attain God-realisation through the instrument of a healthy and strong body.

### II

Germs cause disease when one's vitality comes to a low ebb. They are present even in healthy people. Great doctors have made great researches. When the results of their research tally with those of others, they place before the public their experiences and conclusions arrived at only after repeated experiments. There may be some errors here and there, but they correct them immediately. The germ is not a false imaginary thing.

No system is perfect. Nature Cure is only an auxiliary or help in curing a disease. It is not a complete system to cure any kind of disease. It cannot cure each and every disease. It has its own limitations. Cases that are declared hopeless by Nature-cure come to Allopaths for treatment and vice versa. Cases in intense agony and unbearable pain have to be first allayed on the spot by morphia or cocaine before any curative treatment can be administered.

A long operation requires the aid of chloroform, too.

Nature cure does immense good. We can get its help also. Nature cure cannot do much in an emergency, in war emergency in the field, in relieving acute renal colic, in strangulated hernia and in bullet wounds. Naturopaths depend upon enema for cleaning and hate purgatives. An enema can clean only a small portion of the lower and large intestines. How is the upper portion to be cleaned? An enema cannot penetrate there. This can only be cleansed by a mild laxative. A frequent repetition of drastic purgative may damage the mucus membrane. A mild laxative is highly beneficial.

You can get help from Naturopathy. Naturopathy is a way of living, but at times it develops into a fad. Adjust your diet. Have milk fast. Take an all-fruit diet for some days. Sometimes take milk and fruits. Take to walking, Asanas, mild breathing exercises, stopping short of fatigue. If you do not find much improvement, take some medicines to get rid of the amoeba, etc. Use your discretion.

To undergo Naturopathic treatment by living on fruits is very costly. Further, it is very difficult to undergo this treatment. The mind revolts to fast continuously and to live on fruits. He who has controlled his tongue and is extremely patient can alone practise Nature Cure.

He who undergoes Nature Cure becomes unfit for Sannyasa. Everywhere he has to carry his bag of fruits. If he takes accidentally a little salt or chilli, his whole system is upset as it has become very sensitive and delicate. He cannot live on Bhiksha, which is generally of a mixed character.

Have full fast on Ekadasi. Give up food and water totally. On Sundays give up salt, sugar, chillies, tamarind. Live on milk, curd, fruit. For a week live on fruits alone, an all fruit diet. For a week live on milk alone, an all milk diet. For a week live on three things alone, dhall, rotti, and vegetables. For a week live on vegetables only. For a week live on milk and fruits. For four days fast completely, but drink plenty of water. For a week have restricted diet. For a week take ordinary food. Finally stick to one kind of diet, viz., the restricted diet. At intervals of two or three months have short fasts, all fruit diet, all milk diet, for some days. Such a sort of training is an all-round training and discipline for the tongue.

### III

Do not become a faddist or a slave to some fad. A faddist is intensely or hopelessly or terribly attached to his own pet weak theories or beliefs. A Yogic student or an Allopath or a Naturopath or a philosopher has his own fads. He will never listen to other people's arguments, however cogent, convincing, sound and strong they may be. A faddist develops intolerance and bigotry, which make his mind callous and hard and thus prevent his intellect from vibrating harmoniously to receive others' views. No healthy useful ideas of other schools of thought can ever enter his mind. He takes up one idea from other schools and tries to refute it through clumsy and untenable arguments. Abandon faddism or faddishness. Become very, very catholic, liberal and tolerant in your views. Have a large heart. Give room in your heart for every school of thought and derive benefit from it.

May God bless you all with health, long life, peace, prosperity and Kaivalya!

## RULES FOR PRESERVATION OF HEALTH

Pure atmospheric air is composed of nitrogen, oxygen and a very small proportion of carbon-acid gas. Air once breathed loses the chief part of its oxygen, and acquires a proportionate increase of carbon-acid gas. Therefore, health requires that fresh air should be breathed always.

The solid parts of our bodies are continually wasting, and require to be replaced by fresh substances. Therefore, food, which is to repair the loss, should be taken with due regard to the exercise and waste of the body.

## HEALTH AND HAPPINESS

The fluid parts of our body waste constantly; there is but one fluid in the body which is water. Therefore, water is very necessary, and no artifice can produce a better drink. The fluid of our body is nine to one in proportion to the solid. A like proportion should prevail in the total amount of food taken.

Light exercises have an important influence upon the growth and vigour of the body and the plants. The dwellings should freely admit the solar rays.

Decomposing animal and vegetable substances yield various noxious gases which enter the lungs and corrupt the blood. All impurities should be kept away from dwelling abodes, and every precaution be observed to secure a pure atmosphere.

Warmth is essential to all the bodily functions. Therefore an equable bodily temperature should be maintained by exercise, by clothing, or by fire. Exercise warms, invigorates and purifies the body, clothing preserves the warmth the body generates; fire imparts warmth externally. To obtain and preserve warmth, exercise and clothing are preferable to fire. Fire consumes the oxygen of the air, and produces noxious gases. Therefore, the air is less pure in the presence of candles, gas or coal fire, than otherwise, and the deterioration should be repaired by increased ventilation.

The skin is a highly organised membrane, full of minute pores, cells, blood-vessels, and nerves; it imbibes moisture or throws it off, according to the state of the atmosphere and the temperature of the body. It also breathes, as do the lungs, though less actively. All the internal organs sympathise with the skin. Therefore it should be always kept healthy.

Late hours and anxious pursuits exhaust the nervous system, and produce disease and premature death. Therefore, the hours of labour and study should be short.

Mental and bodily exercises are equally essential to general health and happiness; therefore labour and study should succeed each other.

Man will be most healthy upon simple solids and fluids, of which a sufficient but temperate quantity should be taken;

therefore, strong drinks, tobacco, snuff, opium and all indulgences should be avoided.

Sudden alterations of heat and cold are dangerous, especially to the young and the aged. Therefore, clothing in quantity and quality should be adopted to the alternations of night and day and of the season. Also drinking cold water immediately after coming from the hot sun, and hot tea and soup after bathing in cold water, are productive of many evils.

Moderations in eating and drinking, short hours of labour and study, regularity in exercise, recreation and rest, cleanliness, equanimity of temper and equability of temperature—these are the great essentials to that which surpasses all wealth, viz., health of mind and body.

## HOW TO KEEP HEALTHY

1. Get up at 4 a.m. and do Japa and meditation. Go to bed at 10 p.m. Before sleeping also do Japa. Always repeat God's Name. Entertain pure thoughts. Have a calm, cheerful mind always. Observe Brahmacharya.

2. In the morning take some exercise regularly. Asanas or Suryanamaskaras or walking. Also do deep breathing. Take sun-bath.

3. Avoid tea, coffee, liquors, smoking, tobacco, condiments, spices, rich food, excess of sweet, fried articles, etc.

4. When constipated, take enema or a laxative.

5. A spoonful of honey daily is good. If possible, chew a few neem or bael leaves daily. Take tomatoes, spinach (palak) and plantains regularly. Milk and fruits are good. If milk does not agree with you, take buttermilk.

6. *Very Important:* Eat when you are really hungry. Before eating, offer the food to God and take it as His Prasad. At the end also, pray to Him. Eat in a calm mood; observe Mauna. Eat slowly and masticate thoroughly. Eat moderately. Get up from your seat, when there is still hunger. There should not be any heaviness after a meal.

Do not drink water with food. There should be no exertion (physical or mental) just before and after food. Do not sleep after food, nor bathe. (If possible, do not sleep in daytime at all.) Starches should not be eaten with proteins or acid fruits. Avoid too many items in a meal. Eat simple, light Sattvic food. After a meal sit on Vajrasana for at least 15 minutes, relax thoroughly and do pleasant contemplation on God.

In the morning eat nothing for two or three hours. Finish your evening meal three hours before sleep.

**Drink water:** on getting up from bed
before sleeping
one glass an hour before and after meal
freely at other times.

(An adult needs about six glasses of water in a day).

7. **Ideal Menu:** At 9 a.m. a cup of milk or buttermilk, or juice of a lemon or orange or tomato in a glass of water.

At noon light, Sattvic food. In the afternoon, one or two fruits.

At night (7 or 8 p.m.) milk or buttermilk, fruits and vegetables.

**FAST ON EKADASI.** If you cannot observe complete fast, take fruit juice. Take enema. Drink plenty of water.

Once a week take only fruits and milk twice in the day.

You will enjoy health, long life, vigour and peace of mind also. You will be able to do rigorous Sadhana and attain God-realisation in this very birth.

**MAY GOD BLESS YOU !**

Om Om Om

## THE CAUSE OF AILMENTS AND THE CURE

Impure, weak, vitiated blood is often the foremost cause of all kinds of ailments. The skin, liver and kidneys secrete the unwanted, impure part of the blood. Impure blood is thrown into the lungs every second and is purified by the fresh air breathed in. Therefore, one of the chief conditions of keeping the blood healthy is to breathe always fresh, pure air. One should always exhale as thoroughly as he can. Exhale, exhale and exhale. So that, you could breathe deep more air into the lungs. Next comes cleanliness. The skin must be bathed, cleansed and rubbed dry daily at least once in winter and twice or more in summer. Oil bath should be taken on every alternate day or at least twice a week. The skin should be rubbed vigorously, so that the pores will be open to throw out all impure secretions. Then the kidneys, the liver and the bowels should be kept healthy. They must function properly, and the bowels should be cleared at regular intervals. Many people have pimples on the face or on the body. This is due to humour in the blood. To eradicate this the bowels must be kept always free by regular exercise; avoiding hot, pungent articles and taking plenty of natural laxatives as vegetables, etc., through the practice of Uddiyana and Nauli. Plenty of water should be taken frequently to keep the kidneys healthy so that impure secretions can be thrown out through urine. Practise Paschimottanasana, Padahasthasana, Vajrasana and Mayurasana. The liver and the bowels will function wonderfully. You will have rich, vigorous, pure, healthy blood, and will enjoy a disease-free long life.

## USE YOUR COMMON-SENSE

You must carefully observe the details of your health, particularly its reactions to your diet. Milk is easily digestible to some, whereas it causes retching to some others. Certain kinds of vegetables are suitable to some systems but they may be quite disagreeable to others. The power of digestion varies from person to person. Therefore, you must discriminate between the right food-articles suitable to your constitution and the wrong ones which may cause great harm to your health. Over and above this, you should select only a Sattvic diet, and have moderation in eating, sleeping, etc. Forego your night meals—which should not be taken after 8 p.m.,—once a week, and observe complete fasting once a fortnight. This will give rest to the digestive system, and the assimilative power will be renovated.

Regulate the hours of your sleep, which should not be more than six hours when you are in good health. This can be reduced even to five hours if you do not have much physical fatigue, or heavy mental strain. Midday nap should be completely avoided by children and young persons. If you have the habit of working very late into the night, an hour's nap during the day will refresh you. Use your common-sense always.

Mental health is the first requisite of physical health. Avoid jealousy, envy, hatred and dislike. Do not harbour the spirit of revenge. Forget and forgive. Do not fret within yourself and torment your mind by anger. Do not allow yourself to be pulled down by disappointments and despondence. Let your common-sense guide you: by harbouring jealousy or hatred you practically cause no harm to those you dislike; the spirit of revenge scathes the mind, anger disturbs the peace, and despondence shatters the nerves. Remember that "Even this will pass away". "Nothing indeed is permanent", "All indeed is a mocking show of Maya". Then these negative qualities will take leave of you. Entertain holy thoughts, be of good cheer, light-hearted and keen-minded. Discriminate at every step. You will have wonderful mental health, and consequently a vigorous, disease-free, strong physic.

## BACK TO NATURE

Weakness is sin.
Sin is due to ignorance.
Disease is due to ignorance.
Therefore, attain knowledge or wisdom.
Most diseases are due to modern civilisation.
Blood pressure, pyorrhoea
Are the products of modern civilisation.
Lead a simple, natural life.
Avoid complexities.
There is no necessity for vitamin complex.
Go back to nature.
Mother nature will make you healthy and wise.
Her rules are very simple.
Her fee is nothing.
Her healing herbs and factors are
    abundant, potent and cheap:
Suryanamaskaras, Asanas, Pranayamas,
Japa, Kirtan, Meditation,

Buttermilk, tomato juice,
Lemon juice, sound sleep, walking, running,
Pure air, pure water, wholesome simple food.

## SIMPLE NATURE CURE

The root cause of all diseases is sin against Nature or violation of the laws of nature. The antidote for sin is penance. Therefore, natural treatment (external and internal) for any disease should be some form of penance (Tapasya).

*External treatment:* If there is pain in any part of the body, which is bearable, then a cold water pack may be applied. If the pain is unendurable, then a hot water pack may be applied once or twice a day with an interval of two hours.

*Short fast:* Fast is a curative measure of the greatest importance. By ceasing to take the usual food, the sufferer opens up the way of the Nature's process of elimination of the disease. A short fast should be undertaken as follows:

You should take only the juice of a lemon, orange or Mosambi, in a glass of water three or four times a day.

Such a fast can be observed without the help of any expert or a doctor for three days. During the Naturopathic treatment, daily use of enema to clear the bowels is most essential.

For minor ailments, this kind of fast may be observed for one or two days.

*All-fruit diet:* This should follow the fast and should extend over a week, i.e., twice the number of days of the fast. Take three meals a day of fruits available in the market, except banana. Drink plain water mixed with a juice of a lemon, or orange. If you fast for a day only, you should remain on this fruit diet for two days.

*Fruit and milk diet:* You should have your three meals of fruits as mentioned above, but with the addition of one or two cups of milk at each meal.

If the all-fruit diet is taken only for two days, then this fruit-and-milk diet can be taken for four days.

Thus, the general treatment for some chronic ailment will be as follows for a week:

| | |
|---|---|
| Short fast for | 1 day |
| All-fruit diet for | 2 days |
| Fruit and milk diet for | 4 days |
| **TOTAL** | **7 days** |
| If the short fast is for | 2 days, then |
| The All-fruit diet should be for | 4 days and |
| The fruit-and-milk diet for | 8 days |
| **TOTAL** | **14 days** |

Diseases of long standing require this kind of treatment for at least four to eight weeks.

For common cold or fever, observe a fast for a day or two and fruit diet also for a day or two; and then have your morning meal as usual but evening meal should consist of fruits for one or two days more.

The use of enema is essential in Naturopathic treatment and even, in the state of health, if it is taken every week or at least once a fortnight, it will ward off future troubles, which arise through our own faults.

Fruits and vegetables are nature's remedies to cure diseases. Instead of using costly medicines and injections, we can follow this treatment at home. But, much *patience* is required on the part of the *patient,* because Nature's processes are slow but sure, while medicines suppress the disease rapidly, but the disease raises its head again and again as it is not eradicated. Cheap fruits of the season can be used; then the cost of this Naturopathic treatment will not be more than the cost of medicines and doctor's fees.

If possible, morning and evening, you should take a long walk and it is a simple but the best exercise.

Diseases and difficulties arise whenever we are far from God. God wants then to reestablish our close contact with Him and our full faith in Him. Diseases remind us of the mysterious power of God, and compel us to remember Him and give us a golden opportunity of repeating His name. You may follow any treatment; but Namopathy should invariably form part of the treatment. Namopathy is Japa or repetition of His Name. That is the panacea for all ills.

## INFLUENCE OF THOUGHTS ON HEALTH

Thoughts have power and force. They are powerful like Rama's arrows (Rama Baanam). They hit the target and return to the person who sends them. They have forms also, though they cannot be seen. Good and noble thoughts have very pleasant forms; while evil thoughts have very unpleasant and piercing forms.

Men are Gods in the becoming. If we harbour always thoughts about the good and God, we will surely become good and ultimately God Himself. It is by the Grace of God that we live and work and have our being. Birth and death, pleasure and pain, name and fame, are all dependent upon our actions in the past and the present. God is not responsible for our happiness or our misery. He is just and also kind; and so we cannot blame Him for our misfortunes. Hence, it follows that we should always entertain good thoughts and be calm and cheerful even in difficulties. God does not wish that we should be wise and enlightened, if need be, through unhappiness. Difficulties help us to build our character and so we should face them boldly.

Our mental equilibrium is broken if we allow the thoughts about cares, worries, anxieties, fear, hatred, lust, etc., to enter the mind and if we ponder over them. We have no power to alter the circumstances and environments according to our wishes. But we can change our own mental attitude. We can live in a mental world of our own, and carry on our Sadhana for God-realisation. Therefore, it is of no use dwelling on thoughts about the evil that exists around us. In reality, there is no evil on this earth; it is all our own imagination only. Out of the so-called evil good often cometh.

"A sound mind in a sound body". If our mind is always sound and cheerful, our body cannot be unhealthy because the body is controlled by the mind. Diseases arise first in pessimistic thoughts which react on our bodies. We must gird up our loins to conquer the misfortunes which we have to face. If we always have thoughts about God and our bright future, misfortunes will vanish soon; and we will not feel their impact if we are optimistic.

The thoughts or imaginary fears about diseases or impending evils react upon our bodies and bring on diseases. The right way to live is then to love all, hate none, have no fear, have full faith in God, pray to Him, and remember His Name always. If you do this, you will not feel the pangs of disease or distress and will get power to overcome them. Half the miseries of the world owe their origin to evil thoughts.

Love all. Serve the needy. Meditate on God and you will realise God. Watch your thoughts often and give a good turn to them. Always try to be cheerful and make others happy. Saints have a past; sinners have a future.

## SOIL AND ITS INFLUENCE ON HEALTH

The exterior portion of the earth that is capable of being observed and examined is termed the "crust of the earth", surface soil, or humus. The condition of the interior earth is a matter of mystery even to eminent geologists. Underneath the surface soil is the subsoil and rocky stratum underlies the subsoil.

The constituents of the soil are: mineral matters of various descriptions as clay, limestone, chalk, sand, granite, peat, etc., which predominate in the subsoil and the rocky stratum, organic substances, vegetable and animal, living or dead air in the soil (ground air) and water in the soil (ground water).

The air in the soil varies in amount with the nature of the soil in accordance to the density. It is very impure and moist. It is characterised by an increase in the amount of carbonic acid gas and a diminution in oxygen. It is very rich in organic effluvia. Microbes flourish best in damp soils impregnated with decaying organic matter, and the ground air serves as a medium to carry upwards with it these microbes from their breeding places. If the floor of the house is not rendered absolutely impervious, the ground air which is charged with poisonous effluvia, ascends and supplies the various apartments; Malaria, typhoid fever and yellow fever result.

## SOIL AND ITS INFLUENCE ON HEALTH

Ground water is derived chiefly from rain and partly from the water flowing on the deeper layers of the ground on the surface of impermeable rock by capillary attraction. The ground or subsoil water commences at the lowest limit of the ground air, i.e., at a level where there is a complete exclusion of air in the soil. The depth at which ground water lies varies widely and is influenced by the rainfall. In some places it can be obtained from just below the surface, while in other localities it cannot be traced until several hundreds of feet are sounded. The ground water will be poisoned, if the neighbouring cesspools dug in pervious soils are not rendered impermeable.

The diseases that are caused by the water in the soil are cholera, dysentery, diarrhoea and typhoid fever. The rise of the ground water makes a place damp and causes rheumatic affection, diseases of the lungs as consumption, pneumonia, etc.

Impermeable rocks as granite are considered healthy. Gravel and chalk are also healthy. Clay and marshy soils are unhealthy; but the disadvantages can best be removed if measures are adopted to drain the water readily and effectively. Porous soils should be condemned as they are prone to organic infection. Alluvial soils are unhealthy. Too much stress cannot be laid on the importance of perfect healthiness of a site selected for building purposes. From the standpoint of sanitation, it is highly objectionable to erect a dwelling upon a "made-soil" or "made-land", which is an artificial ground prepared by filling up of hollows and depressions by the deposit of miscellaneous rubbish and especially of organic refuse. But in urban localities, circumstances may arise, and very often do arise, to necessitate recourse to this ground for the erection of a building. In such cases, no building should be erected until the lapse of a sufficient number of years—say four or five years. The underlying principle is that organic matters should be rendered innocuous by free-oxidation and the purifying influence of rain, and finally the made-soil is purified and acquires a healthy nature. Sites for the erection of buildings should admit free circulation of air and free access of sunlight. Sandstone is healthy, because it absorbs water readily but allows it to percolate through and dries rapidly.

It is a matter of difficulty for individuals to have their own choice of soil for their place of residence. In towns, especially, one could not even dream of a free choice of soil. Removal to healthier sites entails grave difficulties, seriously affects the financial problem and as such it is needless to mention that whatever geological condition is afforded had to be availed gladly and made use of to the best advantage. Moisture, i.e., dampness, and foul organic matter that is undergoing decomposition are the two sources of unhealthiness.

The former condition may be obviated by surface and subsoil drainage. The rain water is not permitted to sink but is carried away by proper channels. Subsoil drains serve to lower or remove subsoil water. Raising the level of the ground, and rendering the floor absolutely impermeable are right steps in this direction.

## INFLUENCE OF COLOUR ON HEALTH

Chromotherapy is treatment by colour, which is very simple and potent.

Colour exercises great influence on your health. It has a decided influence on your health. It has a decided influence on your mental states and sense of well-being.

There is psychological influence of colours on account of their associations. Black and sombre colours suggest funerals and so have a depressing effect. Bright colours exercise a cheering influence because of their association with festivity and gaiety. Children jump in joy when they see festoons.

Light-rays are totally reflected by white and totally absorbed by black. Red, blue, green and other colours absorb all rays except those of their own colour.

Green is the king of colours. It is a mild sedative. It is soothing and relieves pain. It is made up of blue and yellow. It preserves and strengthens the eye-sight. It exercises a very soothing influence on the eyes and brain. It is useful in inflammations of the womb, hysteria, etc., cancers, weeping eczema. In sexual irritability and involuntary seminal discharges, the green light is used over the back and the lower spine.

# INFLUENCE OF COLOUR ON HEALTH

Blue contains the chemical or actinic rays. It is a better sedative than the green. It relieves pain. It is a local anaesthetic, too. The blue light is useful in all fevers, in cases of excessive menstrual flow, in skin diseases, old ulcers.

Violet increases the red cells of the blood. It produces sleep in nervous conditions. It is useful in acute cases of tuberculosis.

Orange is a warm colour. Red-orange is the warmest of all. It is very beneficial in stimulating the blood and the nerves.

Red is a warming colour. It gives the thermal rays. It is a nerve stimulant. It is beneficial in chronic rheumatism, bronchitis, dysmenorrhoea, impotency and advanced cases of consumption. It is a great tonic.

Yellow is a healthy colour. It is laxative, and diuretic. It is useful in stimulating the brain, liver and spleen. It is beneficial in paralysis, impotency, syphilis, eye-diseases and constipation.

Indigo is a mixture of warming red and the cooling blue. It is beneficial in advanced cases of consumption, leucorrhoea, hydrocele, disorders of the stomach and womb.

When light enters a room the walls of which are dark in colour, a considerable part of the incoming light is absorbed by the walls. The person who lives in such a room will be living under a very dark shadow. He will be almost deprived of the influence of light.

On the contrary, if a person lives in a room the walls of which are white or nearly white and which hence reflect, instead of absorb, a large part of the brilliant rays. He will be surrounded by a volume of reflected or diffused light. The absence of direct sunlight will be in a large degree compensated for.

Colours may be used externally. For external use the direct rays of the required colour are used. Sometimes, mustard, linseed or olive oil is irradiated and the irradiated substance is rubbed on the skin. For internal use, water and other liquid foods are irradiated and the irradiated articles are taken by the mouth.

Sunlight may be strained by placing colour filters or glasses between the patient and the sun. In the absence of sunlight ordinary lamp may be used. A colour-light-bath is given in an incandescent light Bath Chamber which has lamps of different colours and scientifically arranged switches. Whatever colour irradiation is needed for the patient, lamps of that colour are immediately fixed on to the chamber. The patient removes his clothing, and sits inside the chamber. All the lights are then turned on and the chamber door is closed. The exposure lasts for 5 to 20 minutes, according to the condition of the patient. The wall reflections distribute all the light evenly to all parts of the body of the patient.

## HOW TO BECOME A CENTENARIAN?

Do not worry. Never be in a hurry. Do not eat what you call quick lunches. Take nutritious food. Sleep seven hours a day. Never fool with doctors and do not go into a drugstore except to get a stamp or to consult the directory. When you reach the age of ninety years, you may do as you please.

Wear loose collars, because tight collars present obstacles to the free circulation of the blood through the thyroid gland. Take large quantities of milk, this being the extract of various glands. Remain as much as possible in the open air and especially in the sunshine, and take plenty of exercise, taking care to breathe deeply and regularly. Take a bath daily and in addition once a week or every two weeks take a Turkish or vapour bath. Wear porous clothing, light head-dress and low shoes.

Go early to bed and rise early. "Early to bed and early to rise makes a man healthy, wealthy and wise". Sleep in a very dark, very quiet room and with a window open, and do not sleep less than six or more than seven and a half hours. Give up alcohol. Be temperate in the use of tea or coffee. Avoid places that are overheated, especially by steam, and badly ventilated.

## THE BEST

God is the best Doctor.
Mother Nature is the best physician.
Ganga water is the best drink.
Pranayama is the best exercise.
Brahmacharya is the best tonic.
Mango is the best fruit.

Spinach and Parwal are the best vegetables.
Buttermilk is the best drink for health.
Fasting is the best medicine.
Meditation is the best divine elixir.
Nature-cure is the best cure.
Raw vegetable food is the best food.

## SONG OF VIBHUTI YOGA

(Thars: *Sunaja*)

Bhajo Radhe Krishna
Bhajo Radhe Shyama ...
I am spinach among leafy vegetables,
I am almond among all nuts,
Milk am I among perfect foods,
Tomatoes am I among all vegetables.
I am potatoes among tuber and roots,
I am Basumati rice among all cereals,
Soya bean am I among all pulses,
Cow's ghee am I among all fats,
I am mango among all kinds of fruits.
I am "Alphonso" among all mangoes,
Buttermilk am I among all beverages,
Glucose am I among all sugars.
I am phosphorus among all minerals.
I am vitamin C among all vitamins,
Lady's finger am I among green vegetables,
Barley water am I among invalid foods,
I am first class Protein milk among all proteins,
I am white sugar among carbohydrates,
Turnip am I among English vegetables,
Lemon Juice am I among anti-scorbutics.

## TACT AT THE CHEMIST'S

"Some medicine please", said the young man with the highly refined articulation.

"Yes, sir" smiled the assistant. "What kind, Sir?"

"Fact is", the young man confessed, "I have forgotten. If you wouldn't mind wunning ovah the names of a few things you stock, I should wecognise it at once, howevah. It's quite an easy word I think".

The assistant looked sad. "What is it required for?" he asked.

"To cuah her of cohs", explained the young man in surprise.

"Yes, but the trouble? What is the ailment?"

"Ah! The doctah called it—ah—some kind of itis. I wanna think. Let me see. Yes, it was something in the head with an itis. That's it. Thought I'd get it. I can't remember the whole of the silly name myself, but you will know it."

The assistant stared helplessly.

"Got some teeth out, don't you know", pursued the young man, "and let the cold in... haw, haw!" he broke off, "wathah good that, don't you know. Got some teeth taken out to let the cold in. Took the teeth out to make woom for the cold. See? Jolly good that! Didn't mean it eithaw, 'pon my wo'd."

"Inflammation of the gums" suggested the assistant. "peridentitis, perhaps?"

"By Jove, that's the beggah! Knew we should get it between us. Got into the jaw, don't you know, and developed into asbestos in the mouth. Had to be lanced, don't you know. Had to wun and fetch the doctah, at midnight. Beastly nuisance!"

"Ah an abscess. Very painful thing."

"Wathah! Milly skeweamed a bit. I say, by Jove, I have just wemembah'd the medicine. It's tabloids."

"Yes" encouraged the assistant.

"Tabloids, don't you know. In five gwain doses. Thought I should get it soon."

"Most tabloids are in five grain doses."

"Ah!"

"And many medicines are in tabloid form."

The young man drooped. "How about calomel?" he asked.

"Never heard of it being prescribed for peridentitis."

"Sounded awfully like it. Let me see calomel in pwint, will

you? No, doesn't look weight somehow. Awful squint in my mind's eye, don't you know. Beastly nuisance."

The assistant yawned.

"I say, let's walk round the shop and look at all the difwent tabloids. What's those?"

"Cascara Sagrada."

"Seem to have met him at Coven! Ga'den. Eh what? Not him."

"Phenacetin?"

"Wong again. I say, what a lot of silly things you keep. Do people use'em all?"

"That's the fellow? Knew it as soon as you mentioned him. Do me up a few bottles of that, will you? Thought we should get at the staff with a bit of tact. Useful thing, tact, eh?"

"But Salol would never be used for peridentitis".

"Milly said Salol, I sweah".

"Well, it cannot be peridentitis, sir. Must be liver complaint".

"By Jove, that't it ! Milly didn't want me to talk about—about things like that—to a stwanjah. That was clevah, I don't think.... By Jove, what tact! Eh what? One-and-nine?" Thanks.

## DOMESTIC MEDICINE CHEST

1. Acetic acid
2. Boric acid or Boric powder
3. Alum powder
4. Bicarbonate of soda
5. Easton's syrup
6. Essence of ginger
7. Essence of peppermint
8. Liquid extract of cascara
9. Glycerine
10. Honey
11. Liniment of iodine
12. Tincture of iodine
13. Oil of turpentine

14. Boric ointment
15. Chrysophonic ointment
16. Zinc ointment
17. Vaseline
18. Strong solution of ammonia (Liquor ammonia fortis)
19. Permanganate of potash
20. Sal volatile or (Spiritus ammonia aromaticus)
21. Wine of Ipecac
22. Citrate of caffeine
23. Phenacetin
24. Subnitrate of bismuth
25. Aromatic chalk powder
26. Dover's powder
27. Calomel
28. Chlorodyne
29. Gregory's powder
30. Sweet spirit of nitre
31. Opodeldoc or soap liniment
32. Peregoric
33. Quinine
34. Strong tincture of ginger
35. Magnesium Citrate, granular, effervescent
36. Epsom or glauber's salt
37. Compound Jalap-powder.